JIRA 6.x Administration Cookbook

Over 100 hands-on recipes to help you efficiently administer, customize, and extend your JIRA 6 implementation

Patrick Li

[PACKT] enterprise

PUBLISHING

professional expertise distilled

BIRMINGHAM - MUMBAI

JIRA 6.x Administration Cookbook

First published: July 2014

Production reference: 1030714

Published by Packt Publishing Ltd.
Livery Place
35 Livery Street
Birmingham B3 2PB, UK.

ISBN 978-1-78217-686-2

www.packtpub.com

Cover image by Michal Jasej (milak6@wp.pl)

Credits

Author

Patrick Li

Reviewers

Ed Letifov

Felix Martineau

Ravi Sagar

Mizan Ali Sayed

Commissioning Editor

Vinay Argekar

Acquisition Editor

Vinay Argekar

Content Development Editor

Rikshith Shetty

Technical Editors

Shubhangi H. Dhamgaye

Humera Shaikh

Ritika Singh

Copy Editors

Sarang Chari

Mradula Hegde

Project Coordinators

Melita Lobo

Wendell Palmer

Proofreaders

Simran Bhogal

Ameesha Green

Paul Hindle

Indexers

Rekha Nair

Tejal Soni

Production Coordinators

Kyle Albuquerque

Conidon Miranda

Cover Work

Kyle Albuquerque

About the Author

Patrick Li is the co-founder of, and a senior engineer at, AppFusions. AppFusions is one of the leading Atlassian experts specializing in integration solutions with many enterprise applications and platforms, including IBM Connections, Jive, Google Apps, Box, and SugarCRM.

Patrick has worked in the Atlassian ecosystem for over nine years, developing products and solutions for the Atlassian platform and providing expert consulting services. He has authored numerous books and video courses covering JIRA 4, 5, and 6.

He has extensive experience in designing and deploying Atlassian solutions from the ground up and customizing existing deployments for clients across various industries, such as healthcare, software engineering, financial services, and government agencies.

I would like to thank my wife, Katherine, who has supported and encouraged me along the way, especially while adapting to our new life in San Francisco. I would also like to thank all the reviewers for their valuable feedback, and also the publishers/coordinators for their help in making this book happen.

About the Reviewers

Ed Letifov, Atlassian Expert, has been in IT for 17 years.

Originally from Russia, though born in the last decade of the Soviet Union era, he's been moving around for the last 14 years, has been employed by various international companies, and has worked with clients on five different continents.

His first encounter with JIRA was in 2003, and he still remembers shaking hands with the Atlassian founding fathers at the time when Atlassian was a "cute, small start-up down under" ready to take on the world.

Atlassian was and remains one of the very few companies he has worked for for any length of time, if only he hadn't discovered New Zealand.

He is the co-founder of TechTime Initiative Group—an accredited Atlassian Expert in New Zealand. Through their TurningRight Service for "all products Atlassian", he provides support, maintenance, implementation, and custom development services to the government, educational institutions, and commercial organizations in New Zealand and worldwide.

Ed's favorite activity is problem solving and solution design. His endless personal quest is for "a product he can identify with", and he's been looking for it in the fields of automatic personal task planning and voice-driven programming.

He mixes this quest with volunteering at various community organizations, playing basketball and bass guitar (usually not at the same time), and writing poetry (whenever inspiration strikes).

In a world of search engines, wikis, and instant knowledge of dubious quality, he still loves the feel of a good book in his hand.

Ed can be contacted at LinkedIn (`http://nz.linkedin.com/in/edletifov/`), LiveJournal (`http://techtime.livejournal.com/`), or through his company websites—TurningRight (`http://turningright.co.nz`) and TechTime (`http://techtime.co.nz`).

Felix Martineau runs the Atlassian Practice at TechSolCom and has a rare blend of deep IT expertise, people skills, and business acumen. While he thinks of himself as a jack-of-all-trades, he has developed world-class JIRA expertise. A recognized player in the Atlassian community, Felix is a regular contributor to top JIRA plugins and has been involved with several JIRA books.

Felix started using JIRA in 2007, and what started out as purely technical expertise evolved into Business Process Management, Enterprise Collaboration, Application Lifecycle Management, Agile Methodology, change management, and personal productivity. Nowadays, he works to bring JIRA outside of IT and make it a household name for business users. A confessed self-improvement geek, Felix is always looking for ways to improve and take on new challenges.

I want to thank the people at Packt for giving me the opportunity to review this book; it's been a pleasure!

I would also like to thank my girlfriend, Genevieve, for her unwavering support, and everybody who is on my team: friends, colleagues, mentors, and of course, my family.

Ravi Sagar is a Drupal and JIRA expert with over 11 years of experience in Web Development and Business Analysis. He has done extensive work implementing and customizing big JIRA instances for Issue and Project Tracking, Test Management with JIRA, Support Tickets, and Agile Tracking.

Ravi founded Sparxsys Solutions Pvt. Ltd. (www.sparxsys.com) in 2010—a start-up company that provides consultancy and training services in Drupal and JIRA/Agile.

He also writes a lot about technology and entrepreneurship on his blog, www.ravisagar.in, and loves photography and running marathons.

You can connect with him at http://www.linkedin.com/in/ravisagar or e-mail him at ravi@sparxsys.com

Mizan Ali Sayed works as an Atlassian tools specialist with eQuest Technologies (http://www.equestind.com), and has experience in implementing, customizing, and supporting Atlassian tools, chiefly JIRA and Confluence. Mizan has a good blend of technical expertise, people skills, and troubleshooting skills. He is active within the Atlassian community and has published free add-ons on the Atlassian Marketplace. You can reach him at mizanalisayed@gmail.com.

www.PacktPub.com

Support files, eBooks, discount offers and more

You might want to visit www.PacktPub.com for support files and downloads related to your book.

Did you know that Packt offers eBook versions of every book published, with PDF and ePub files available? You can upgrade to the eBook version at www.PacktPub.com and as a print book customer, you are entitled to a discount on the eBook copy. Get in touch with us at service@packtpub.com for more details.

At www.PacktPub.com, you can also read a collection of free technical articles, sign up for a range of free newsletters and receive exclusive discounts and offers on Packt books and eBooks.

http://PacktLib.PacktPub.com

Do you need instant solutions to your IT questions? PacktLib is Packt's online digital book library. Here, you can access, read and search across Packt's entire library of books.

Why Subscribe?

- Fully searchable across every book published by Packt
- Copy and paste, print and bookmark content
- On demand and accessible via web browser

Free Access for Packt account holders

If you have an account with Packt at www.PacktPub.com, you can use this to access PacktLib today and view nine entirely free books. Simply use your login credentials for immediate access.

Instant Updates on New Packt Books

Get notified! Find out when new books are published by following @PacktEnterprise on Twitter, or the *Packt Enterprise* Facebook page.

Table of Contents

Preface

Atlassian JIRA is an enterprise issue-tracker system. One of its key strengths is its ability to adapt to the needs of an organization, right from the frontend of a user interface to providing a platform for add-ons to extend its capabilities. However, understanding its flexibility and picking the right add-ons can often be a daunting task for many administrators. Learning how to take advantage of JIRA's power while keeping the overall design simple and clean is important for the success of its implementation and future growth.

This book is full of useful recipes with real-life JIRA administration challenges, solutions, and examples. Each recipe contains easy-to-follow, step-by-step instructions, and illustrations from the actual application.

What this book covers

Chapter 1, *JIRA Server Administration*, contains recipes that will help you to administer your JIRA server, including installing, upgrading, and securing JIRA with SSL certificates.

Chapter 2, *Fields and Screens*, contains recipes that let you customize JIRA with custom fields and screens. This chapter also includes advanced techniques such as using scripts and add-ons to add more control to fields that are not available with JIRA.

Chapter 3, *JIRA Workflows*, covers one of the most powerful features in JIRA, with recipes that show you how to work with workflows, including permissions and user input validation. This chapter also covers workflow bundling and using scripts to extend out-of-the-box components.

Chapter 4, *User Management*, explains how users and groups are managed within JIRA. It starts with simple recipes to cover out-of-the-box user management features, and goes on to include topics such as LDAP integration and various single sign-on implementations.

Chapter 5, *JIRA Security*, focuses on the different security control features offered by JIRA, including different levels of permission and authorization control. This chapter also covers other security-related topics, such as the user password policy and capturing electronic signatures.

Chapter 6, E-mails and Notifications, explains JIRA's e-mail handling system for both outgoing and incoming e-mails. This chapter also covers JIRA's event system and how to extend the basic set of events and templates.

Chapter 7, Integrating with JIRA, covers how to integrate JIRA with other systems, including other Atlassian applications and many other popular cloud platforms, such as Google Drive and GitHub.

Chapter 8, JIRA Administration, covers a broad range of recipes that help to make administrative tasks easier and simpler. It includes problem troubleshooting, task automation, and general scripting.

Chapter 9, JIRA Customizations, covers other user JIRA customization recipes to improve overall usability such as content translation, project cloning, and configuration migration.

What you need for this book

For installation and upgrade recipes, you will need to have the latest JIRA 6 distribution, which you can download directly from Atlassian at `http://www.atlassian.com/software/jira/download`.

You may also need several additional software, including the following:

▶ Java SDK: You can get this at `http://java.sun.com/javase/downloads`
▶ MySQL: You can get this at `http://dev.mysql.com/downloads`

Who this book is for

JIRA 6.x Administration Cookbook is intended for administrators who will be customizing, supporting, and maintaining JIRA for their organizations.

You will need to be familiar with and have a good understanding of JIRA's core concepts. For certain recipes, a basic understanding of HTML, CSS, and JavaScript will also be helpful.

Conventions

In this book, you will find a number of styles of text that distinguish between different kinds of information. Here are some examples of these styles, and an explanation of their meaning.

Code words in text, database table names, folder names, filenames, file extensions, pathnames, dummy URLs, user input, and Twitter handles are shown as follows: "Take your current JIRA offline, for example, by running the stop `jira.bat` script."

A block of code is set as follows:

```
<Connector port="8443" maxHttpHeaderSize="8192" SSLEnabled="true"
maxThreads="150" minSpareThreads="25" maxSpareThreads="75"
enableLookups="false" disableUploadTimeout="true"
acceptCount="100" scheme="https" secure="true"
clientAuth="false" sslProtocol="TLS" useBodyEncodingForURI="true"/>
```

New terms and **important words** are shown in bold. Words that you see on the screen, in menus or dialog boxes for example, appear in the text like this: "Type in the target system's address in the **Rules** text box."

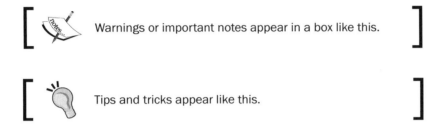

Warnings or important notes appear in a box like this.

Tips and tricks appear like this.

Reader feedback

Feedback from our readers is always welcome. Let us know what you think about this book— what you liked or may have disliked. Reader feedback is important for us to develop titles that you really get the most out of.

To send us general feedback, simply send an e-mail to feedback@packtpub.com, and mention the book title via the subject of your message. If there is a topic that you have expertise in and you are interested in either writing or contributing to a book, see our author guide on www.packtpub.com/authors.

Customer support

Now that you are the proud owner of a Packt book, we have a number of things to help you to get the most from your purchase.

Downloading the example code

You can download the example code files for all Packt books you have purchased from your account at http://www.packtpub.com. If you purchased this book elsewhere, you can visit http://www.packtpub.com/support and register to have the files e-mailed directly to you.

Errata

Although we have taken every care to ensure the accuracy of our content, mistakes do happen. If you find a mistake in one of our books—maybe a mistake in the text or the code—we would be grateful if you would report this to us. By doing so, you can save other readers from frustration and help us improve subsequent versions of this book. If you find any errata, please report them by visiting http://www.packtpub.com/submit-errata, selecting your book, clicking on the **errata submission form** link, and entering the details of your errata. Once your errata are verified, your submission will be accepted and the errata will be uploaded on our website, or added to any list of existing errata, under the Errata section of that title. Any existing errata can be viewed by selecting your title from http://www.packtpub.com/support.

Piracy

Piracy of copyright material on the Internet is an ongoing problem across all media. At Packt, we take the protection of our copyright and licenses very seriously. If you come across any illegal copies of our works, in any form, on the Internet, please provide us with the location address or website name immediately so that we can pursue a remedy.

Please contact us at copyright@packtpub.com with a link to the suspected pirated material.

We appreciate your help in protecting our authors, and our ability to bring you valuable content.

Questions

You can contact us at questions@packtpub.com if you are having a problem with any aspect of the book, and we will do our best to address it.

1
JIRA Server Administration

In this chapter, we will cover:

- ▸ Installing JIRA for production use
- ▸ Upgrading JIRA with an installer
- ▸ Upgrading JIRA manually
- ▸ Migrating JIRA to another environment
- ▸ Setting up the context path for JIRA
- ▸ Setting up SSL
- ▸ Installing SSL certificates from other applications
- ▸ Resetting the JIRA administrator password
- ▸ Generating test data in JIRA
- ▸ Anonymizing JIRA exports

Introduction

Atlassian JIRA is a popular issue-tracking system used by many companies across the world. One of its strengths, unlike most other enterprise software, is it does not take days or weeks to install and implement, and it is very simple to upgrade and maintain.

We will assume that you, the reader, already know how to install a brand new JIRA. So, we will explore common administration tasks, such as upgrading and migrating your JIRA, looking at different options, from using the new automated upgrade utility provided by Atlassian to doing everything from scratch.

We will also look at some other neat tricks you can do as an administrator, such as resetting the admin password to get you out of sticky situations.

Installing JIRA for production use

In this recipe, we will look at how to install and set up JIRA in a production environment. This includes setting up a dedicated user to run JIRA under and using an external database.

We will be using the standalone archive distribution, as the steps are consistent across both Windows and Linux platforms.

Getting ready

The following things need to be checked before you start with this recipe:

- Download the latest JIRA archive distribution from `https://www.atlassian.com/software/jira/download` and click on the **All JIRA Download Options** link.
- Make sure your server environment meets JIRA's requirements by visiting the following link: `https://confluence.atlassian.com/display/JIRA/Supported+Platforms`.
- Install Java on the system. At the time of writing, JIRA 6 required Java 7. Make sure you get the latest update for Java, unless it is explicitly stated as unsupported by JIRA.
- Make sure the `JAVA_HOME` or `JRE_HOME` environment variable is configured.
- Have a database system available, either on the server hosting JIRA or a different server accessible over the network. For this recipe, we will be using MySQL; if you are using a different database, change the commands and queries accordingly.
- Download the necessary database driver. For MySQL, you can download it from `https://dev.mysql.com/downloads/connector/j`.

How to do it...

We first need to create an empty MySQL database for JIRA:

1. Open up a new command prompt on the MySQL server.
2. Run the following command (you can also use another user instead of root as long as the user has permission to create new users and databases):

   ```
   mysql -u root -p
   ```

3. Enter the password for the user when prompted.

4. Create a new database for JIRA by running the following command:

```
create database jiradb character set utf8;
```

5. Create a new user for JIRA in the database and grant the user access to the `jiradb` database we just created using the following command:

```
grant all on jiradb.* to 'jirauser'@'localhost' identified by
'jirapassword';
```

In the previous five steps, we have created a new database named `jiradb` and a new database user named `jirauser`. We will be using these details later to connect JIRA with MySQL. The next step is to install JIRA.

6. Create a dedicated user account to run JIRA under. If you're using Linux, run the following command as root or with sudo:

```
useradd --create-home --comment "Dedicated JIRA account" --shell /
bin/bash jira
```

 It is a good practice to reduce security risks by locking down the user account so that it does not have login permissions.

7. Create a new directory on the filesystem where JIRA will be installed in. This directory will be referred to as `JIRA_INSTALL`.

8. Create another directory on the filesystem. This will be used for JIRA to store its attachments, search indexes, and other information. You can create this directory on a different drive with more hard disk capacity, such as a network drive (this could slow down the performance). This directory will be referred to as `JIRA_HOME`.

 It is a good practice to keep the `JIRA_INSTALL` and `JIRA_HOME` directories separate, that is, the `JIRA_HOME` directory should not be a subdirectory inside `JIRA_INSTALL`. This will make future upgrading and maintenance easier.

9. Unzip the JIRA archive file in the `JIRA_INSTALL` directory.

10. Change both the `JIRA_INSTALL` and `JIRA_HOME` directories' owner to the new JIRA user.

11. Open the `JIRA_INSTALL/atlassian-jira/WEB-INF/classes/jira-application.properties` file in a text editor.

12. Locate the `jira.home=` line in this file.

13. Cut and paste this in the full path to the `JIRA_HOME` directory and remove the # symbol if present. Make sure you use the forward slash (/). The following line shows how it looks on a Linux system:

    `jira.home=/opt/data/jira_home`

> Windows uses the backward slash (\) in the file path. You should still use the forward slash (/) while specifying the `jira.home` directory.

14. Copy the database driver JAR file to the `JIRA_INSTALL/lib` directory.

15. Start up JIRA by running the `start-jira.sh` (for Linux) or `start-jira.bat` (for Windows) script from the `JIRA_INSTALL/bin` directory as the JIRA user.

    JIRA comes with a setup wizard that will help guide us through the final phase of the installation.

16. Open up a browser and go to `http://host:8080`. By default, JIRA runs on port 8080. You can change this by changing the connector port value in the `JIRA_INSTALL/conf/server.xml` file.

17. The first step is to select the language JIRA will use for its user interface.

18. The second step is to set up the database information. Select the **My Own Database (recommended for production environments)** option.

19. Select a value for the **Database Type** option. For this recipe, select the **MySQL** option.

20. Enter the details for our new `jiradb` database.

21. Click on **Test Connection** to check whether JIRA is able to connect to the database.

22. Click on **Next** to move to the second step of the wizard as shown in the following screenshot:

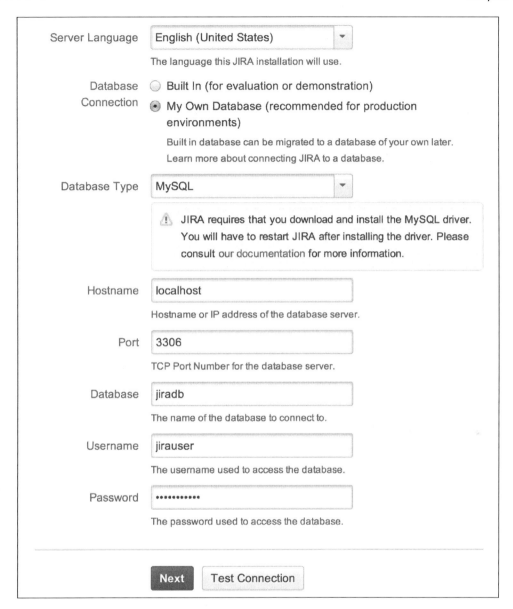

23. Enter the title for this JIRA instance.

24. Select **Public** if you would like to let people sign up for accounts, or select **Private** if you want only administrators to create accounts. For most organizations that use JIRA to track internal projects, it will be the **Private** mode.

25. Set the **Base URL** option. The base URL is the one that users will use to access JIRA. Usually, this should be a fully qualified domain name or the hostname, that is, not a localhost or an IP address.

26. Click on **Next** to go to the third step of the wizard, as shown in the following screenshot:

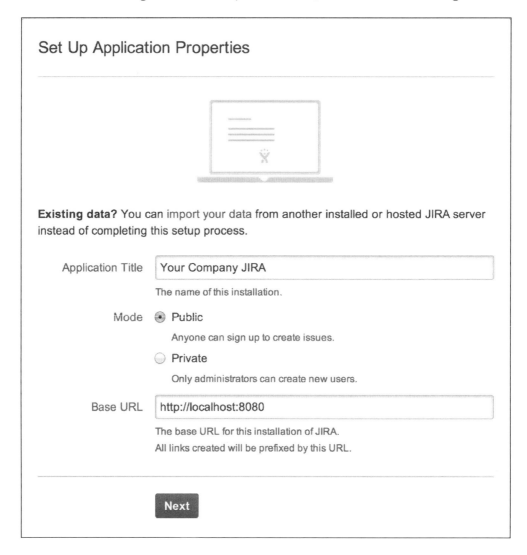

27. Enter your JIRA license key.

28. Select the **I don't have an account** option if you do not have a valid JIRA license and you do not have an account on `my.atlassian.com`.

29. Select the **I have an account but no key** option if you have an account on `my.atlassian.com` but you do not have a valid JIRA license key.

30. Select the **I have a key** option if you have a valid JIRA license key handy.

31. Click on **Next** to go to the fourth step of the wizard, as shown in the following screenshot:

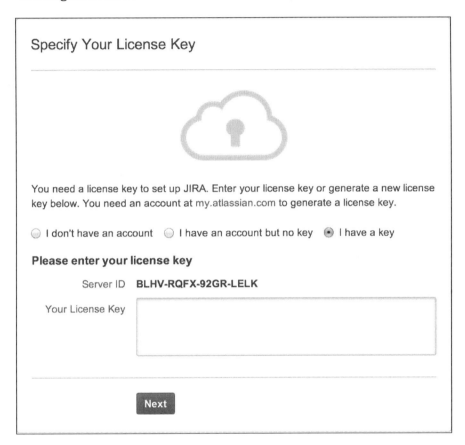

32. Enter the details for the initial administrator account. The user account will have access to all configuration options in JIRA, so make sure you do not lose its login credentials.

33. Click on **Next** to go to the fifth and final step of the wizard, as shown in the following screenshot:

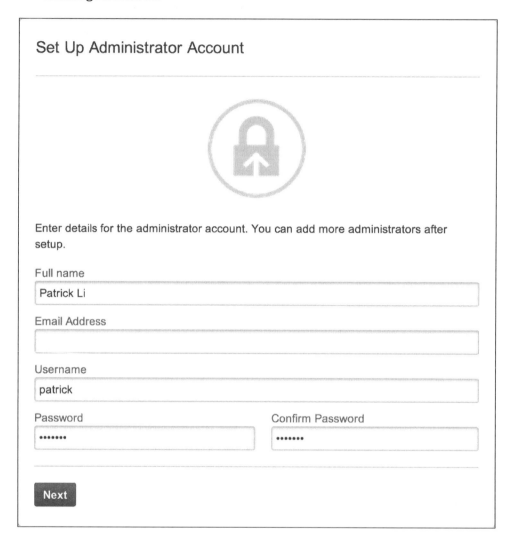

Set Up Administrator Account

Enter details for the administrator account. You can add more administrators after setup.

Full name

Patrick Li

Email Address

Username

patrick

Password

•••••••

Confirm Password

•••••••

Next

34. Choose if you want to set up an outgoing SMTP server now or later. If you do not have an SMTP server ready right now, you can always come back and configure it later.

35. Click on **Finish** to complete the setup process, as shown in the following screenshot:

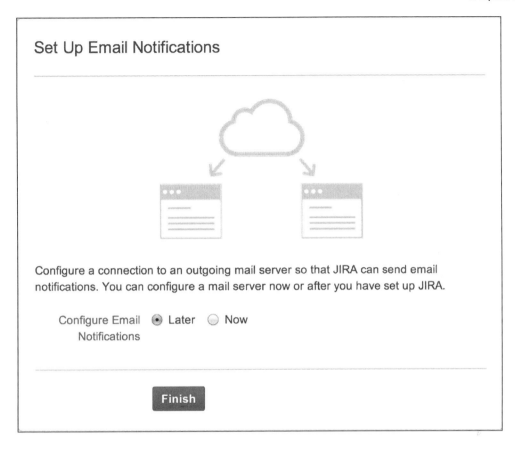

Set Up Email Notifications

Configure a connection to an outgoing mail server so that JIRA can send email notifications. You can configure a mail server now or after you have set up JIRA.

Configure Email Notifications: ● Later ○ Now

Finish

Once JIRA finishes the final setup procedures, you will be automatically logged in with the initial administrator account you created.

There's more...

By default, JIRA is set to use a maximum of 768 MB of memory. For a production deployment, you might need to increase the amount of memory allocated to JIRA. You can increase this by opening up the `setenv.sh` (on Linux) or `setenv.bat` (on Windows) file in the `JIRA_INSTALL/bin` directory and changing the value for the `JVM_MAXIMUM_MEMORY` parameter. For example, if we want to set the maximum memory to 2 GB, we will change it to `JVM_MAXIMUM_MEMORY="2048m"`. You will need to restart JIRA after performing this change. For production uses, it is recommended that you allocate at least 2 GB of memory to the JIRA JVM.

If you are using LDAP for user management in your organization, refer to the *Integrating with LDAP for authentication only* recipe in *Chapter 4, User Management*.

Upgrading JIRA with an installer

In this recipe, we will show you how to upgrade your JIRA instance with the standard JIRA installer.

Getting ready

Since the JIRA installer is only available for standalone installations on Windows and Linux, we will be running you through the installer on Windows for this recipe:

- Check the upgrade notes for any special instructions as well as the target JIRA version to make sure you can perform a direct upgrade.

- Make sure you have a valid JIRA license.

- Verify whether your current host environment is compatible with the target JIRA version. This includes the Java version, database, and operating system.

- Verify whether your operating environment is compatible with the target's JIRA version, specifically the browser requirements.

- Make sure that the add-ons you are using are compatible with the new version of JIRA.

 You can use the Universal Plugin Manager's JIRA update check utility to check for add-on compatibility.

- Download the installer binary for your target JIRA version.

How to do it...

Upgrade your JIRA with the installer using the following steps:

1. Take your current JIRA offline; for example, by running the `stop-jira.bat` script.
2. Back up the JIRA database with its native backup utility.
3. Launch the installer and select the **Upgrade an existing JIRA installation** option.
4. Select the directory where the current JIRA is installed:

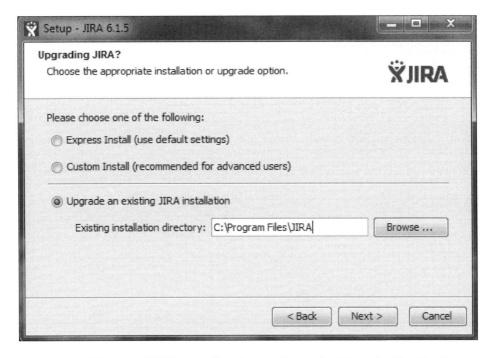

5. Check the **Back up JIRA home directory** option and click on the **Next** button.

6. Review the upgrade checklist and click on the **Upgrade** button:

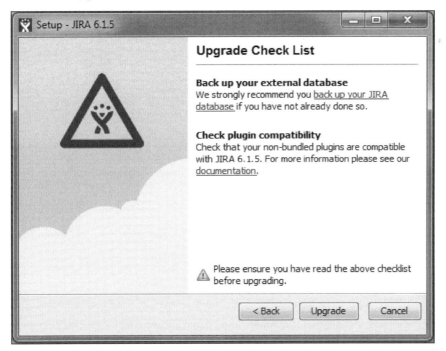

7. Wait for the installer to complete the upgrade process. Once the upgrade is complete, the installer will automatically launch JIRA.

8. Update add-ons once JIRA has successfully started.

The installer will detect and provide you with a list of customized files in the `JIRA_INSTALL` directory, which you will need to manually copy after the upgrade.

See also

If you cannot use the installer to upgrade JIRA, refer to the *Upgrading JIRA manually* recipe.

Upgrading JIRA manually

If you find yourself in a situation where you cannot use the JIRA installer to upgrade JIRA, for example, you are hosting JIRA on an OS that does not have an installer binary such as Solaris, or if you are using the WAR distribution, then you need to manually upgrade your JIRA instance.

Getting ready

The general prerequisite tasks for upgrading JIRA manually will remain the same as that of the installer. Refer to the previous recipe for the common tasks involved. Since the installer automates many of the backup tasks while upgrading JIRA manually, you will have to do the following:

1. Back up the JIRA database with its native backup utility

2. Back up the `JIRA_INSTALL` directory

3. Back up the `JIRA_HOME` directory

4. Get a list of all the customized files in the `JIRA_INSTALL` directory from the System Info page in JIRA

5. For the WAR distribution, prepare and configure the installation files

How to do it...

To manually upgrade your JIRA instance, perform the following steps:

1. Take your current JIRA offline.

2. Install the new version of JIRA.

3. Edit the `jira-application.properties` file in this version of JIRA, located in the `JIRA_INSTALL/atlassian-jira/WEB-INF/classes` directory.

4. Update the value of `jira.home` to the current `JIRA_HOME` directory or to a copy of that directory.

5. Copy any modified files.

6. Start up the new JIRA.

7. Update the add-ons once JIRA starts successfully.

8. Remove the previous installation directory to avoid confusion.

How it works...

What we are doing here is essentially setting up a new instance of JIRA and pointing it to the old JIRA's data. When we start up the new JIRA, it will detect that the database it is connecting to contains data from an older version of JIRA by reading the `dbconfig.xml` file from the `JIRA_HOME` directory. It will also proceed to make all the necessary schema changes.

Migrating JIRA to another environment

Now that we have gone through upgrading a JIRA instance, we will look at how to move a JIRA instance to another server environment. This is a common use case when you need to move an application to a virtualized environment or data warehouse.

Getting ready

The following things need to be checked before you start with this recipe:

- Make sure you have a valid JIRA license.
- Check whether your new environment is compatible with JIRA system requirements.
- Ensure both the old and new JIRA are of the same major or minor version. If you intend to run a newer version of JIRA in the new environment, it is recommended that you upgrade after the migration is successful.

 Migrating a system can be very disruptive for users. Make sure you communicate this to your users and allocate enough time for rollbacks.

How to do it...

To migrate an existing JIRA to another server, perform the following steps:

1. Download and install a brand new JIRA instance in your new environment with an empty database.

2. Take your current JIRA offline.

3. Back up your current JIRA database with its native backup utility.

4. Back up your current `JIRA_HOME` directory.

5. Take your new JIRA offline.

6. Copy over your `JIRA_HOME` backup and replace the new `JIRA_HOME` directory with it.

7. Update the `dbconfig.xml` file with the new JIRA database details.

8. Copy your database backup and restore the new JIRA database.

9. Start up the new JIRA.

 If you have made modifications to your JIRA configuration files, you can get a complete list of the modified files from JIRA's **System Info** page.

10. Log in to JIRA as a JIRA administrator.

11. Select **System Info** from the **Administration** panel.

12. Note down the files listed in the **Modified Files** and **Removed Files** sections.

13. Review and apply the same changes to the new JIRA instance.

The following screenshot shows how the output will look:

Modified Files	[Installation Type: Standalone] jira-application.properties, WEB-INF/web.xml
Removed Files	[Installation Type: Standalone] There have been no removed files

Setting up the context path for JIRA

If you have multiple web applications running on the same domain, you might want to set up a context path for JIRA; for example, `http://example.com/jira`.

How to do it...

Perform the following steps to set up a context path for JIRA:

1. Shut down JIRA if it is running.
2. Open up `JIRA_INSTALL/conf/server.xml` in a text editor.
3. Locate the following line and enter the context path for the path attribute, for example, `path="/jira"`:

    ```
    <Context path="" docBase="${catalina.home}/atlassian-jira"
    reloadable="false" useHttpOnly="true">
    ```

4. Save the file and restart JIRA.

    If you have updated the context path for JIRA after it is installed, you will have to update JIRA's **Base URL** option so that all its links will reflect the change.

5. Log in to JIRA as an administrator.
6. Navigate to **Administration | Systems | General Configuration**.
7. Click on the **Edit Settings** button.
8. Enter the fully qualified URL into JIRA, including the context path in the **Base URL** field.
9. Click on **Update** to apply the change.

After you have all this set up, you will be able to access JIRA with the new context path.

Setting up SSL

By default, JIRA runs with a standard, nonencrypted HTTP protocol. This is acceptable if you are running JIRA in a secured environment such as an internal network. However, if you plan to open up access to JIRA over the Internet, you need to tighten up the security by encrypting sensitive data, such as the usernames and passwords that are being sent, by enabling **HTTP over SSL** (**HTTPS**).

This recipe describes how to install SSL on the JIRA Tomcat application server. If you have an HTTP web server such as Apache in front of JIRA, you can install the SSL certificate in the web server instead.

Getting ready

You need to have the following set up before you can step through this recipe:

- ▶ Obtain a valid SSL certificate. You can either use a self-signed certificate or obtain one from a **Certificate Authority** (**CA**) such as VeriSign. Using a self-signed certificate will display a warning message when users first visit the site, as shown in the following screenshot:

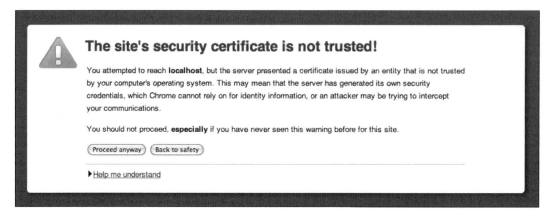

- ▶ Ensure that the JAVA_HOME environment variable is set properly.
- ▶ Make sure you know which JDK/JRE JIRA is using. You can find this information from the **System Info** page, where you need to look for the java.home property.
- ▶ Make sure your JRE/JDK's bin directory is added to your PATH environment variable, and the keytool command will output its usage, as shown in the following screenshot:

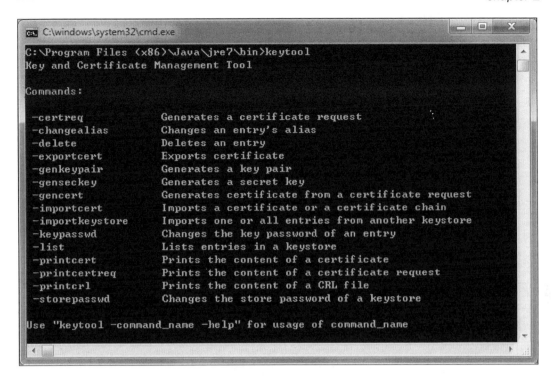

How to do it...

Perform the following steps to import an SSL certificate:

1. Open up a command window and go to the directory where the certificate file resides.

2. Generate a **Java KeyStore** (**JKS**) for JIRA by running the `keytool -genkey -alias jira -keyalg RSA -keystore JIRA_INSTALL/jira.jks` command.

3. Import the certificate into KeyStore by running the `keytool -import -alias jira -keystore JIRA_INSTALL/jira.jks -file file.crt` command, where `file.crt` is the certificate file.

4. Open the `server.xml` file located in the `JIRA_INSTALL/conf` directory in a text editor.

5. Locate and uncomment the following XML configuration snippet:

```
<Connector port="8443" maxHttpHeaderSize="8192"
  SSLEnabled="true"
maxThreads="150" minSpareThreads="25" maxSpareThreads="75"
enableLookups="false" disableUploadTimeout="true"
acceptCount="100" scheme="https" secure="true"
clientAuth="false" sslProtocol="TLS"
  useBodyEncodingForURI="true"/>
```

Downloading the example code

You can download the example code files for all Packt books you have purchased from your account at http://www.packtpub.com. If you purchased this book elsewhere, you can visit http://www.packtpub.com/support and register to have the files e-mailed directly to you.

6. Add a few new attributes to the Connector tag and save the file:

```
keystoreFile="PATH_TO_YOUR_KEYSTORE"
keystorePass="PASSWORD_FOR_YOUR_KEYSTORE"
keyAlias="jira"
keystoreType="JKS"
```

7. Restart JIRA to apply the changes.

How it works...

We first created a new Java KeyStore for JIRA to store its own SSL certificate with Java's keytool utility. During this step, you are prompted to provide information about the certificate as well as a password to access KeyStore.

 Do not lose the password to KeyStore.

After we created KeyStore, we imported the certificate and then enabled an additional connector to listen for HTTPS connections by uncommenting the connector XML tag. We also added new attributes to the tag so that Tomcat will know where our new KeyStore is and how to access it to get to the certificate.

You can also change the port number for the connector if you want to run HTTPS on the more common port 443 instead of the default 8443, and your final XML snippet will look something like the following:

```
<Connector port="443" maxHttpHeaderSize="8192" SSLEnabled="true"
maxThreads="150" minSpareThreads="25" maxSpareThreads="75"
enableLookups="false" disableUploadTimeout="true"
acceptCount="100" scheme="https" secure="true"
clientAuth="false" sslProtocol="TLS" useBodyEncodingForURI="true"
  keystoreFile="/opt/jira/jira.jks" keystorePass="changeme"
keyAlias="jira"
  keystoreType="JKS"/>
```

There's more...

At this point, users can access JIRA with both HTTP and HTTPS, and you need to configure JIRA so that it will automatically redirect all the HTTP traffic to HTTPS. JIRA comes with a handy configuration utility that can help you set up this configuration.

 You should first make sure your HTTPS configuration is working correctly before attempting this recipe.

Note that this utility is only available for standalone installations; if you are running a WAR installation, you can skip the following steps and move on to the manual setup section:

1. Open the command prompt and go to the `JIRA_INSTALL/bin` directory.
2. Depending on your OS, run the `config.bat` or `config.sh` file.
3. Select the **Web Server** tab from the **JIRA Configuration Tool** window.
4. Select the **HTTP and HTTPs (redirect HTTP to HTTPs)** option for **Profile**.
5. Click on the **Save** button at the bottom of the window as shown in the following screenshot.
6. Restart JIRA to apply the change.

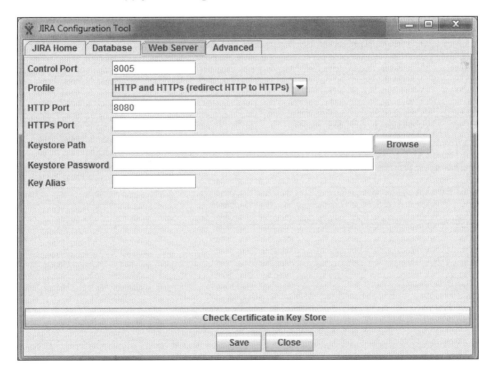

If you cannot use **JIRA Configuration Tool**, you can perform the following steps to manually set up the configuration:

1. Open the `web.xml` file located in the `JIRA_INSTALL/atlassian-jira/WEB-INF` directory.

2. Add the following XML snippet at the end of the file, just before the closing `</webapp>` tag:

```
<security-constraint>
    <display-name>HTTP to HTTPs Redirection</display-name>
    <web-resource-collection>
        <web-resource-name>all-except-attachments</web-
            resource-name>
        <url-pattern>*.jsp</url-pattern>
        <url-pattern>*.jspa</url-pattern>
        <url-pattern>/browse/*</url-pattern>
    </web-resource-collection>
    <user-data-constraint>
        <transport-guarantee>CONFIDENTIAL</transport-
            guarantee>
    </user-data-constraint>
</security-constraint>
```

3. Restart JIRA to apply the change.

See also

For information on connecting JIRA to other applications that run on SSL, refer to the *Installing SSL certificates from other applications* recipe.

Installing SSL certificates from other applications

You might need to connect JIRA to other services such as LDAP, mail servers, and other websites. Often, these services make use of SSL. In such cases, the connection will fail, and you will see the following errors in your JIRA log file:

```
javax.net.ssl.SSLHandshakeException:
sun.security.validator.ValidatorException: PKIX path building
failed:
sun.security.provider.certpath.SunCertPathBuilderException: unable
to find valid certification path to requested target
```

Getting ready

For this recipe, we will be using the Java keytool utility, so make sure you have the following configuration set up:

- ▸ Obtain the SSL certificate from the target system.
- ▸ Ensure that the `JAVA_HOME` environment variable is set properly.
- ▸ Make sure you know which JDK/JRE JIRA is using. You can find this information from the **System Info** page, where you need to look for the `java.home` property.
- ▸ Make sure your JRE/JDK's `bin` directory is added to your PATH environment variable, and the `keytool` command will output its usage.
- ▸ Obtain the password for the Java trust store used by JIRA.

How to do it...

In this recipe, let's assume we want to connect JIRA to an LDAP server that is running on SSL. Perform the following steps to make it a trusted site inside JIRA:

1. Open up a command prompt and go to the directory where the certificate file resides.
2. Import the certificate into the trust store by running the `keytool -import -alias tomcat -file file.cer JAVA_HOME\jre\lib\security\cacerts` command, where `file.cer` is the certificate file.
3. Restart JIRA to apply the changes.

How it works...

When JIRA attempts to connect to an SSL-protected service, it will first determine whether the target service can be trusted by checking if the service's certificate is present in what is called the **trust store**. If the certificate is not present, the connection will fail.

The trust store is typically a KeyStore called `cacerts` and is located in the `$JAVA_HOME/lib/security` directory on the server.

We used the keytool utility to import the certificate to our local trust store, so the target service will be registered as a trusted service and allows JIRA to successfully connect to it.

There's more...

Manually downloading the certificate and running the `keytool` command every time can be a hassle. To make life easier for you, there is a free add-on called **SSL for JIRA** from Atlassian Labs that can help you automate some of the steps. You can download this add-on from the following link:

```
https://marketplace.atlassian.com/plugins/com.atlassian.jira.plugin.
jirasslplugin
```

Perform the following steps to use the **SSL for JIRA** add-on:

1. Log in to JIRA as a JIRA administrator.

2. Navigate to **Administration** | **System** | **Configure SSL**.

3. Type in the target system's address in the **Rules** textbox in the `host:port` format (for example, **smtp.gmail.com:465**).

> You can add multiple systems by specifying each one on a new line.

4. Click on **Save certificates** as shown in the following screenshot.

5. Follow the instruction on the screen to copy over the `cacerts` file to the target location.

6. Restart JIRA to apply the changes.

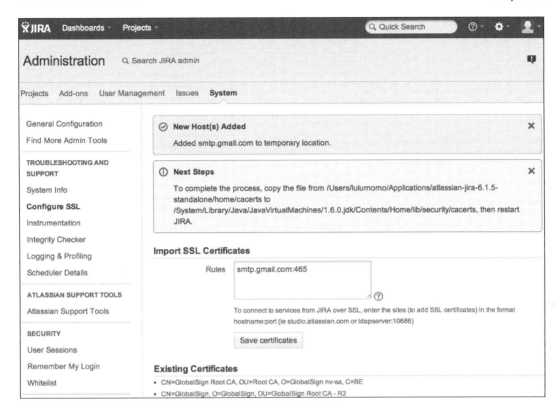

 Do not confuse this add-on with running JIRA over SSL.

Resetting the JIRA administrator password

Sometimes, you might forget or lose the password to the account with the JIRA Administrator or JIRA System Administrator permission, and you cannot retrieve it using the password-reset option. For example, suppose JIRA does not have an SMTP server configured, or you are restoring JIRA from a data dump and do not know the account and/or password. In these cases, you need to reset the administrator password directly in the database.

 This recipe only applies to JIRA instances that use the default internal user directory option. External user management such as LDAP will not work with this recipe.

Getting ready

Since we will reset the password in JIRA's database, make sure you do the following:

▶ Connect to the JIRA database either via the command line or a GUI

▶ Update the JIRA database records

How to do it...

Let's assume we use the default `mysql` command-line tool and **MySQL** as the backend database for JIRA. If you are using a different database, you may need to change the following SQL statements accordingly:

1. Connect to the JIRA database with a client tool by running the `mysql -u jirauser -p` command, where `jirauser` is the username to access the JIRA database.

 You can find JIRA's database details from the `dbconfig.xml` file located at `JIRA_HOME`.

2. Change to the JIRA database by running the `use jiradb` command, where `jiradb` is the name of JIRA's database.

3. Determine the groups that have the JIRA System Administrators global permission with the following SQL statement:

```
select perm_parameter from schemepermissions where
    PERMISSION=44;
```

4. Find users that belong to the groups returned in step 3 using the following SQL statement, where `jira-administrators` is a group returned from step 3:

```
select child_name, directory_id from cwd_membership where
    parent_name='jira-administrators';
```

5. Reset the user's password in the database with the following SQL statement, where `admin` is a user returned in step 4:

```
update cwd_user set
credential='uQieO/1CGMUIXXftw3ynrsaYLShI+GTcPS4LdUGWbIusFvH
PfUzD7CZvms6yMMvA8I7FViHVEqr6Mj4pCLKAFQ==' where
user_name='admin';
```

6. Restart JIRA to apply the change.

How it works...

With JIRA's internal user directory, all the user and group data are stored in the JIRA database. The value `44` is the ID for the JIRA System Administrators global permission.

If you do not know what groups or users have been granted the JIRA System Administrators global permission, we will first have to find this information using steps 3 and 4. Otherwise, you can skip to step 5 in order to reset the password.

JIRA's user password information is stored in the `cwd_user` table. Since JIRA only stores the hash value of the password, we changed the user's `admin` password to `uQieO/1CGMUIXXf tw3ynrsaYLShI+GTcPS4LdUGWbIusFvHPfUzD7CZvms6yMMvA8I7FViHVEqr6Mj4pCLK AFQ==`, which is the hash value of `sphere`.

Generating test data in JIRA

For many production JIRA instances, it is often important to understand how it will perform under an anticipated load, how well it scales as the usage grows, and whether the hardware will be able to support the anticipated growth.

This can be tricky for new installations, as an empty JIRA cannot realistically provide any performance indication. In this recipe, we will look at how we can generate any arbitrary amount of test data to simulate an anticipated data size. For example, we will be able to measure the average response time and how long it takes to reindex the system.

 Use this recipe in your test environment. Do not use this in production.

Getting ready

For this recipe, we need to use the JIRA Data Generator add-on from Atlassian Labs. You can download this add-on at the following link:

`https://marketplace.atlassian.com/plugins/com.atlassian.jira.plugins. jira-data-generator`

How to do it...

Once the add-on is installed in JIRA, perform the following steps to generate test data:

1. Log in to JIRA as a JIRA administrator.

2. Navigate to **Administration | System | Generate Metadata**:

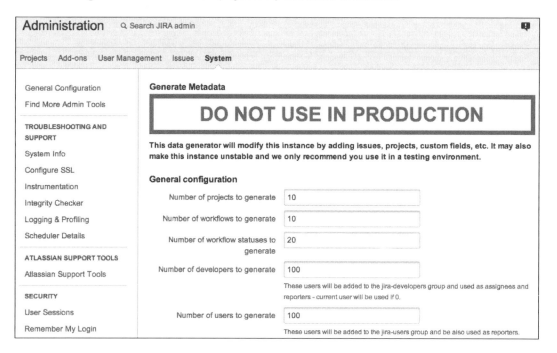

3. Set the number of projects and other metadata to generate.

4. Click on **Generate** and wait for the process to complete.

5. Select **Generate Data**.

6. Set the number of issues, comments, and other data that is to be generated.

7. Click on **Generate** and wait for the process to complete, as shown in the following screenshot:

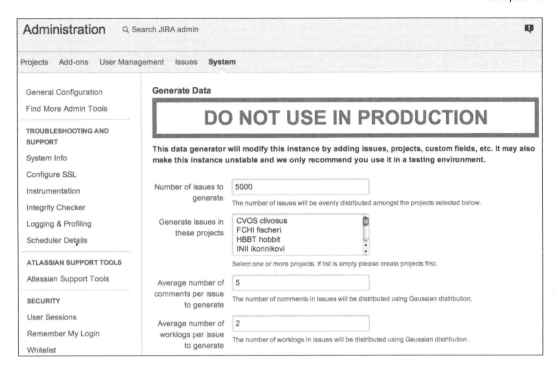

How it works...

Generating test data in JIRA with the JIRA Data Generator add-on is a two-step process. We first need to create all the necessary configuration metadata such as custom fields and workflows and then create the issues.

Anonymizing JIRA exports

Sometimes, in order to troubleshoot your JIRA instance, you need to provide a data dump for Atlassian or another service vendor so that they can recreate your environment to reproduce the problem locally. If you have sensitive information in your JIRA, this can be troublesome. In this recipe, we will look at how we can anonymize our data in JIRA.

Getting ready

For this recipe, we need to use the JIRA Anonymizer utility. You can download it from the following link:

```
https://confluence.atlassian.com/download/attachments/139008/jira_
anon.zip?version=1&modificationDate=1367988226752&api=v2
```

To run the Anonymizer utility, make sure that the following prerequisites are met on the machine you are running the utility from:

- ▶ Make sure the `JAVA_HOME` environment variable is set properly
- ▶ Running the `java -version` command will display the correct version of Java

How to do it...

Perform the following steps to anonymize your JIRA export:

1. Unzip the `jira_anon.zip` file to a temporary directory.
2. Copy your JIRA XML export (`entities.xml`) to the temporary directory.
3. Open up a command prompt and go to the temporary directory where the `joost.jar` file resides.
4. Run the anonymizer application with the `java -Xmx512m -jar joost.jar entities.xml anon.stx > anon-entities.xml` command, where `entities.xml` is the name of the original XML export and `anon-entities.xml` is the new anonymized XML file to be created.

JIRA's XML backup utility produces a ZIP file that contains two XML files; do not anonymize `activeobjects.xml`.

How it works...

The JIRA Anonymizer protects sensitive information in your JIRA by going through your JIRA XML export and replacing values from many fields in JIRA with a string of the character x. The list of fields that are to be anonymized include the following:

- ▶ Issue summary, environment, and description
- ▶ Comments, work logs, and change logs
- ▶ The project description
- ▶ Configuration scheme description such as the notification and permission schemes
- ▶ Attachment filenames
- ▶ Text custom field types

Depending on the size of the export, the utility may require additional memory for processing. The `-Xmx` parameter indicates the amount of memory to allocate, so in the preceding steps, we allocated 512 MB of memory to run the utility.

2
Fields and Screens

In this chapter, we will cover the following topics:

- ▶ Creating a new custom field
- ▶ Creating separate select options for different projects
- ▶ Making a field required
- ▶ Making the assignee field required
- ▶ Hiding a field from view
- ▶ Choosing a different field renderer
- ▶ Creating a new field configuration
- ▶ Creating a new screen
- ▶ Removing the none option
- ▶ Adding help tips to custom fields
- ▶ Using JavaScript with custom fields
- ▶ Creating custom field with custom logic

Introduction

An information system such as Atlassian JIRA is only as useful as the data that goes into it, so it is no surprise that JIRA is very flexible when it comes to letting you customize the fields and screens.

JIRA comes with a suite of default fields to help you get it up and running quickly, and it also allows you to add your own fields, called **custom fields**, to address your unique needs.

In this chapter, we will learn not only about how to create these custom fields in JIRA, but also the different behaviors that these fields can have. We will end the chapter by showing you an example of expanding the types of custom fields you can have with third-party add-ons and using scripts to create your own field logic.

Creating a new custom field

As mentioned before, one of the key features of JIRA is its ability to let you customize the fields in which you have to collect information from the user. JIRA comes with over 20 different types of custom fields, such as simple text and select lists.

In this recipe, we will be creating a new custom field—a single select list custom field—from the default selection.

How to do it...

Proceed with the following steps to create a new custom field of the type single select list:

1. Log in to JIRA as a JIRA administrator.
2. Navigate to **Administration | Issues | Custom Fields**.
3. Click on the **Add Custom Field** button.
4. Scroll down and select the **Select List (single choice)** field type, and click on **Next** as shown in the following screenshot:

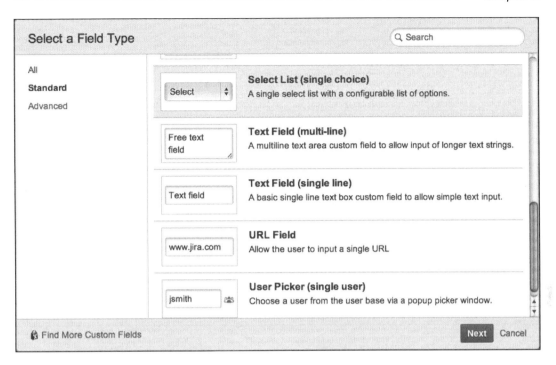

5. Name the custom field `Team`.

6. Add select options by typing the option value in the **Options** text field and click on **Add**. Continue until all options are added and then click on **Next**, as shown in the following screenshot:

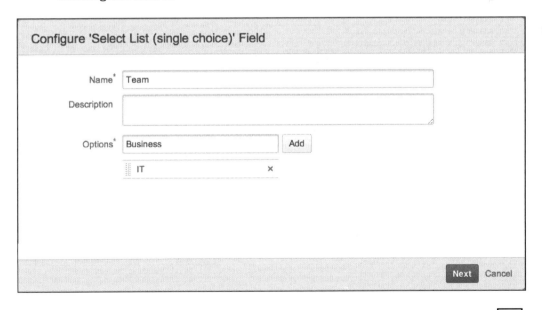

7. Select the screens to place the new `Team` custom field onto, and click on **Update** to finish, as shown in the following screenshot. Note that you can always add the field to other screens later.

Associate field Team to screens

Associate the field Team to the appropriate screens. You must associate a field to a screen before it will be displayed. New fields will be added to the end of a tab.

Screen	Tab	Select
Default Screen	Field Tab	☑
Resolve Issue Screen	Field Tab	☐
Workflow Screen	Field Tab	☐

[Update]   Cancel

 The custom field will only appear on screens that it is associated with.

See also

For select type custom fields, such as single/multi selects, radio buttons, and checkboxes, you can set up separate set of select options for different project- and issue-type combinations. Refer to the next recipe, *Creating separate select options for different projects*.

Creating separate select options for different projects

Often, it is useful for custom fields to have different values depending on the selected project and issue type combination. A good example would be for a select list custom field to show different sets of options for different projects.

We will look at how to achieve this with a **custom field configuration scheme**, also known as **context**. A custom field configuration scheme controls what data the custom field will display, such as the field's default value and select options. Just like all other configuration schemes in JIRA, the custom field configuration scheme is applied on a project and issue type context.

How to do it...

We need to create a new custom field configuration scheme in order to set up a new set of select list options:

1. Log in to JIRA as a JIRA administrator.

2. Navigate to **Administration | Issues | Custom Fields**.

3. Click the **Configure** link for the field configuration used by the project and issue type.

4. Click on the **Add new context** link.

5. Give a name for the new context.

6. Choose **Issue Types** and **Projects** that the new context will be applied to, and click on **Add**.

7. Click the **Edit Options** link for the new context.

8. Add new options and click on **Done** when finished, as shown in the following screenshot:

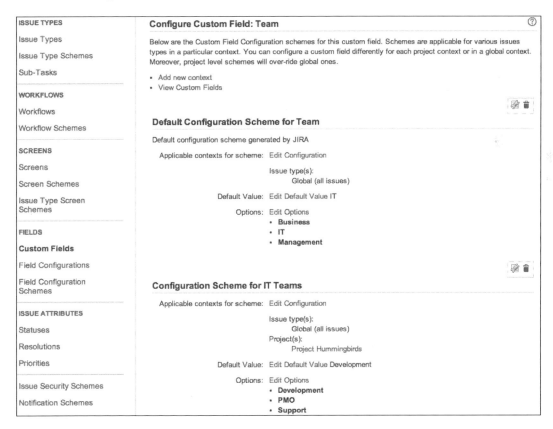

Project specific schemes will override the default scheme.

How it works...

When you are creating or editing an issue, JIRA will look up custom field configuration schemes that are applicable to the current project and issue type selection. The scheme with the most specific project/issue type context will be selected (or **default scheme** will be selected if none is found), and its configurations will be applied for the custom field.

Note that you can only create one context per project. You cannot have different issue type contexts within the same project.

There's more...

As mentioned earlier, you can also set different default values with custom field configuration schemes, so you can have fields pre-filled based on different project and issue type combinations.

Making a field required

Required fields such as **Summary** and **Issue Type** have a little red asterisk next to them, which means they must have a value when you are creating or updating an issue. This is a great way to ensure users will not skip filling in important information.

We will look at how to make any fields of your choice required in this recipe, with **field configurations**. A field configuration controls the behaviors of a field; these include the field's mandatory requirements, visibility, renderer, and description.

How to do it...

Proceed with the following steps to make a field required in JIRA:

1. Log into JIRA as a JIRA administrator.
2. Navigate to **Administration | Issues | Field Configurations**.
3. Click on the **Configure** link for the field configuration used by the project and issue type.
4. Click on the **Required** link for **Priority** and **Due Date** as shown in the following screenshot:

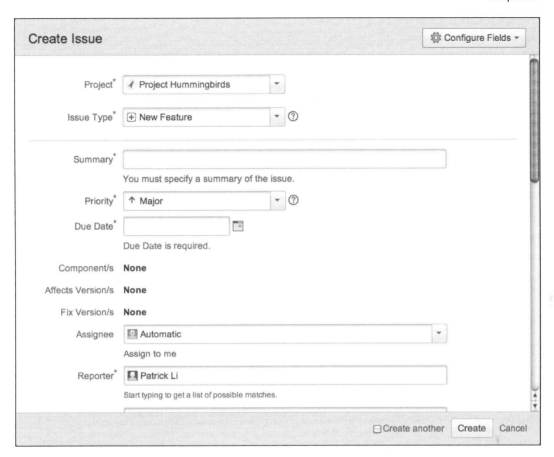

How it works...

When a field is marked as required, JIRA will check to make sure the field has a value when you are making updates to the issue, such as an edit or during a workflow transition. This validation is applied even if the field is not present on the screen, so make sure you do not make a field that is not required on screen, otherwise users will not be able to complete the action.

Certain fields such as **Assignee** and **Due Date** require the user to have certain permissions to make updates. If the user does not have the necessary permissions, the validation will fail and prevent the user from completing the action.

There's more...

Clicking on the **Optional** link will make the field not required. Certain fields such as **Issue Type** must be required.

See also

The *Making the assignee field required* recipe.

Making the assignee field required

By default, the assignee field has an **unassigned** option, which is equivalent to making the field optional. If you went to check out field configuration, you would have realized that you could not make the assignee field required as there is no such option available.

In this recipe, we will look at how to disable the unassigned option, effectively making the assignee a required field.

Getting ready

You cannot disable the unassigned option if you have:

 ▶ Issues that are currently using that option for the assignee field
 ▶ Projects that have unassigned set as the default assignee

How to do it...

Proceed with the following steps to disable the unassigned option:

1. Log in to JIRA as a JIRA administrator.
2. Navigate to **Administration | System**.
3. Click on the **Edit Settings** button.
4. Scroll down and select the **OFF** option for **Allow unassigned issues** and click on **Update**, as shown in the following screenshot:

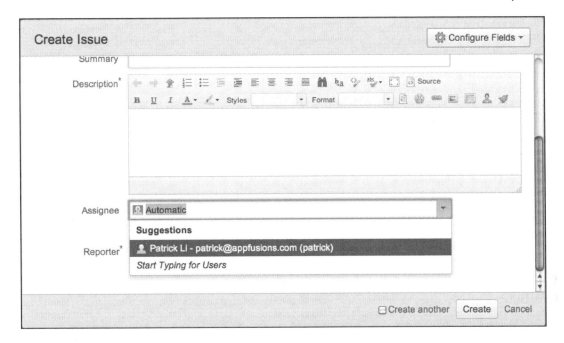

Hiding a field from view

There will be times when a field is no longer needed. When this happens, instead of deleting the field, which would also remove all its data, you can choose to hide it. So if you need the field again further down the track, you can simply unhide it and retain all the data.

In this recipe, we will be hiding both the **Priority** and **Due Date** fields.

How to do it...

Proceed with the following steps to hide a field in JIRA:

1. Log in to JIRA as a JIRA administrator.
2. Navigate to **Administration | Issues | Field Configurations**.
3. Click on the **Configure** link for the field configuration used by the project and issue type.
4. Click on the **Hide** link for **Priority** and **Due Date**.

 Clicking on the **Show** link will unhide the field. You cannot hide a mandatory field.

There's more...

Using field configuration is one way to hide fields from the user. There are two more ways to make a field hidden from view:

- ▶ Take the field offscreen. Note that for the **View** screen, default fields, such as summary and description, are shown regardless of whether they are placed on the screen.

- ▶ Restrict the field's configuration scheme, so it is not applicable to the project/issue type context.

Hiding the field with field configuration will make it hidden from all screens, so if you want to hide the field from specific screens, you should not use field configuration, but simply take the field off the appropriate screens. For example, if you want to make a field read-only after an issue is created, you can simply take it off the screen assigned to the edit issue operation.

Choosing a different field renderer

Most custom field types, such as select lists and text fields, can be rendered in multiple ways. For example, select lists can be rendered either with an autocomplete feature or as a simple, standard drop-down list.

In this recipe, we will be changing the environment field to use **Wiki Style Renderer** so that we can use wiki markup when entering data.

How to do it...

Proceed with the following steps to change the field renderer option:

1. Log in to JIRA as a JIRA administrator.
2. Navigate to **Administration | Issues | Field Configurations**.
3. Click on the **Configure** link for the field configuration used by the project and issue type.
4. Click on the **Renders** link for the field to change.
5. Select the new renderer type from the **Active Renderer** drop-down list.
6. Click on **Update** to apply the change as shown in the following screenshot:

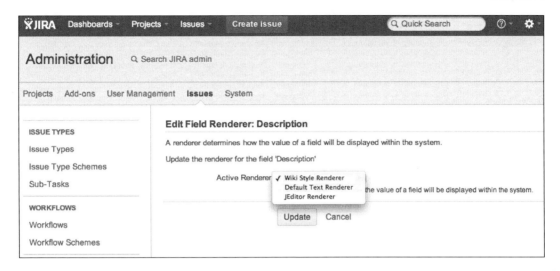

There's more...

JIRA comes with several field renderers to choose from, and you can install custom renderers from third-party vendors. A good example is the JEditor add-on (`https://marketplace.atlassian.com/plugins/com.jiraeditor.jeditor`), which provides a rich text editor for all text-based fields, such as the **Description** field, as shown in the following screenshot:

Creating a new field configuration

As we have seen in previous recipes, you can configure a field's behaviors with field configuration. JIRA not only comes with a default field configuration that is applied to all project and issue types by default, but it also lets you create your own so that you can choose the projects and/or issue types to apply your field configuration to.

In this recipe, we will make the **Description** and **Assignee** fields required only for the **Task** issue type.

How to do it...

Setting up a new field configuration is a three-step process. The first step is to create the new field configurations:

1. Log in to JIRA as a JIRA administrator.

2. Navigate to **Administration | Issues | Field Configurations**.

3. Click on the **Add Field Configuration** button, name it `Task Field Configuration`, and click on **Add**.

4. Click on the **Required** link for **Description** and **Assignee** fields.

The second step is to associate the new field configuration with a new field configuration scheme:

1. Navigate to **Administration | Issues | Field Configuration Schemes**.

2. Click on the **Add Field Configuration Scheme** button, name it `Task Field Configuration Scheme`, and click on **Add**.

3. Click on the **Associate an Issue Type with a Field Configuration** button.

4. Select **Task** for **Issue Type**, **Task Field Configuration** for **Field Configuration**, and click on **Add**, as shown in the following screenshot:

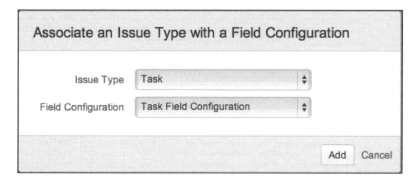

The last step is to apply the new field configuration scheme to our project:

1. Navigate to **Administration | Projects**.

2. Select a project from the list.

3. Select **Fields** from the left-hand side panel.

4. Navigate to **Actions | Use a different scheme**.

5. Select the new **Task Field Configuration Scheme** option and click on **Associate**.

Creating a new screen

JIRA comes with three screens by default—**Default Screen**, **Resolve Issue Screen**, and **Workflow Screen**.

In this recipe, we will look at how to create a new screen from scratch and then make it appear when we are creating a new issue of type **Task**.

How to do it...

The screen is one of the most complicated configurations in JIRA. To create a new screen and apply it often requires you to configure multiple schemes. So we will break these steps into three logical groups.

Firstly, we need to create our new screen:

1. Log in to JIRA as a JIRA administrator.

2. Navigate to **Administration | Issues | Screens**.

3. Click on the **Add Screen** button, name the new screen Task Create Screen, and click on **Add**.

4. Select and add the **Summary**, **Issue Type**, **Description**, **Assignee**, and **Reporter** fields, as shown in the following screenshot:

Secondly, we need to assign the new **Task Create Screen** to the **Create Issue** operation:

1. Navigate to **Administration | Issues | Screen Schemes**.
2. Click on the **Add Screen Scheme** button, name the new screen `Task Screen Scheme`, select **Default Screen** as the **Default Screen** option, and click on **Add**.
3. Click on the **Associate an Issue Operation with a Screen** button.
4. Select **Create Issue** for **Issue Operation**, **Task Create Screen** for **Screen**, and click on **Add**, as shown in the following screenshot:

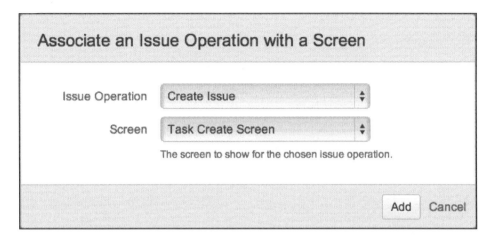

Third, we need to assign the new **Task Screen Scheme** to the **Task** issue type:

1. Navigate to **Administration | Issues | Issue Type Screen Schemes**.

2. Click on the **Add Issue Type Screen Scheme** button, and call the new screen **Task Issue Type Screen Scheme**.

3. Select **Default Screen Scheme** as the **Screen Scheme** option and click on **Add**.

4. Click on the **Associate an Issue Type with a Screen Scheme** button.

5. Select **Task** for **Issue Type**, **Task Screen Scheme** for **Screen Scheme**, and click on **Add**, as shown in the following screenshot:

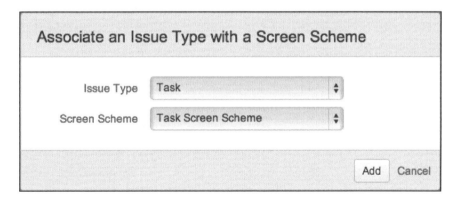

Lastly, we need to apply the new screen **Task Issue Type Screen Scheme** to the project:

1. Navigate to **Administration | Projects**.
2. Select a project from the list.
3. Select **Screens** from the left-hand side panel.
4. Navigate to **Actions | Use a different scheme**.
5. Select the new **Task Issue Type Screen Scheme** and click on **Associate**.

How it works...

The screen is one of the most confusing aspects of JIRA configuration. When we create a new screen, we need to associate it with one of the three issue operations (create, edit, and view) with screen scheme. As in our recipe, we associated our new **Task Create Screen** with the **Create Issue** operation.

Screen schemes then need to be associated with issue types, so that JIRA can determine which screen scheme to use based on the selected issue type.

Lastly, we apply the issue type screen scheme to a project, so only the selected projects will have the screens associated. The following diagram provides a comprehensive illustration of the relationships between screens, fields, and their various schemes:

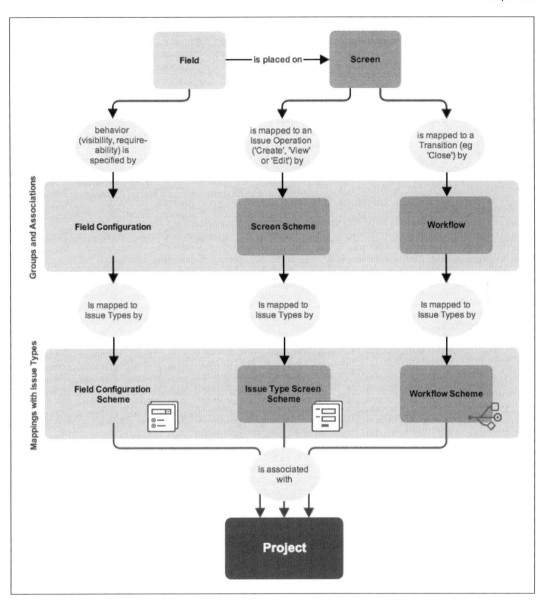

Reference/Credit from https://confluence.atlassian.com/display/JIRA/
Configuring+Fields+and+Screens

Removing the none option

Custom field types such as select list (single and multi) come with the **None** option, and the only way to remove that is to make the field required. While this makes sense, it can be cumbersome to chase down every field and configuration.

In this recipe, we will remove the **None** option from all single select list custom fields.

Getting ready

Since we will be modifying physical files in JIRA, you will want to make backups of the files we change.

How to do it...

JIRA uses Velocity templates to render custom fields. These templates are mostly HTML with some special symbols. You can find all these files in the `JIRA_INSTALL/atlassian-jira/WEB-INF/classes/plugins/fields` directory, and the edit view templates are in the `edit` subdirectory.

So we need to open the `edit-select.vm` file in a text editor and remove the following code snippet:

```
#if (!$fieldLayoutItem || $fieldLayoutItem.required == false)
        <option value="-1">$i18n.getText("common.words.none")</option>
    #else
        #if ( !$configs.default )
        <option value="">$i18n.getText("common.words.none")</option>
        #end
    #end
```

Make sure you *do not* change any other lines, then save the file, and restart JIRA.

> You can remove the **None** option from other custom field types, such as multi-select by editing the appropriate file, for example, `edit-multiselect.vm`.

How it works...

The Velocity `.vm` template files are what JIRA uses to render the HTML for the custom fields. The code snippet we removed is what displays the **None** option. Note that by changing the template, we are removing the **None** option for all single select custom fields in JIRA. If you just want to remove the **None** option for a single custom field, refer to the *Using JavaScript with custom fields* recipe.

Adding help tips to custom fields

Users who are new to JIRA often find it confusing when it comes to filling in fields, especially custom fields. So it is useful for you as the administrator to provide useful tips and descriptions to explain what some of the fields are for.

In this recipe, we will be adding a help icon for the **Team** custom field.

How to do it...

Proceed with the following steps to add help tips to a custom field:

1. Log in to JIRA as a JIRA administrator.
2. Navigate to **Administration | Issues | Custom Fields**.
3. Click on the **Edit** link for the custom field.
4. Enter the following HTML snippets into the **Description** text box, and click on **Update**. You might want to substitute the `href` value to a real page containing help text.

   Need help to work out Team assignment? Try this:

   ```
   <a class="help-lnk" href="/secure/ShowConstantsHelp.
   jspa?decorator=popup#Teams" title="Get help about Team" data-
   helplink="local" target="_blank">
       <span class="aui-icon aui-icon-small aui-iconfont-help"></
   span>
   </a>
   ```

The following screenshot shows our new help icon:

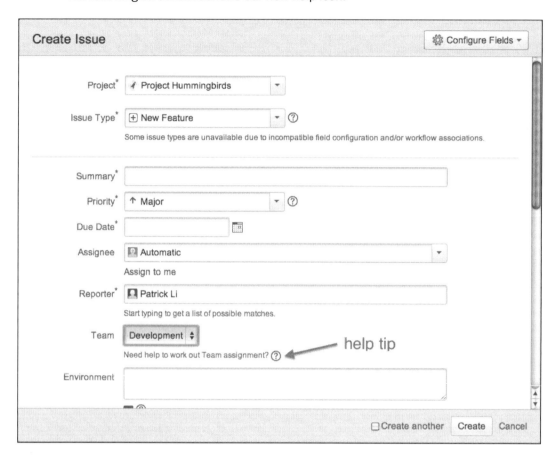

How it works...

JIRA allows us to use any valid HTML for custom field description, so we added a simple text and an anchor tag that links to an HTML page containing our help information. We also added a span tag with the proper style class to have the nice question mark icon used by **Issue Type** and **Priority** fields.

The `data-helplink="local"` attribute for the anchor tag ensures when the user clicks on the help icon; the help page is opened in a separate page rather than redirecting the current page.

 Since the custom field description is rendered as it is, make sure you validate your HTML, for example, close all your HTML tags.

There's more...

Normally, we put descriptions directly into the custom field's description textbox as demonstrated. You can also put your descriptions into the field configuration settings, such as hiding a field. Doing so offers the following advantages:

▶ You can have different help texts for different project/issue type contexts

▶ You can set help texts for fields that are not custom fields, such as **Summary** and **Description**

Proceed with the following steps to set field descriptions in field configuration:

1. Navigate to **Administration | Issues | Field Configurations**.
2. Click on the **Configure** link for the field configuration used by the project and issue type.
3. Click on the **Edit** link for the field.
4. Enter the HTML snippets into the **Description** field and click on **Update**.

See also

Refer to the *Using JavaScript with custom fields* recipe on other tricks you can do with custom field descriptions.

Using JavaScript with custom fields

Just as in the *Adding help tips to custom fields* recipe, we can also add JavaScript code in the custom field description as long as we wrap the code in the `<script>` tags.

In this recipe, we will look at another way to remove the **None** option from select list custom fields.

Getting ready

This recipe uses the jQuery JavaScript library, which is bundled with JIRA. If you are not familiar with jQuery, you can find the documentation at `http://jquery.com`.

We will also need to use the custom field's ID in our script, so you will need to have that handy. You can find the ID by going to the custom fields page, clicking on the **Edit** link of the target field, and clicking the number at the end of the URL is the field's ID. For example, the following URL shows a custom field with the ID `10103`:

```
http://jira.localhost.com:8080/secure/admin/EditCustomField!default.
jspa?id=10103
```

How to do it...

Proceed with the following steps to add JavaScript to custom field description:

1. Log in to JIRA as a JIRA administrator.

2. Navigate to **Administration | Issues | Custom Fields**.

3. Click on the **Edit** link for the custom field.

4. Enter the following JavaScript snippets into the **Description** text box and click on **Update**. You will need to substitute it in your custom field's ID.

```
<script>
AJS.$('#customfield_10103 option[value="-1"]').remove();
</script>
```

The following screenshot shows that the **Team** custom field no longer has the **None** option:

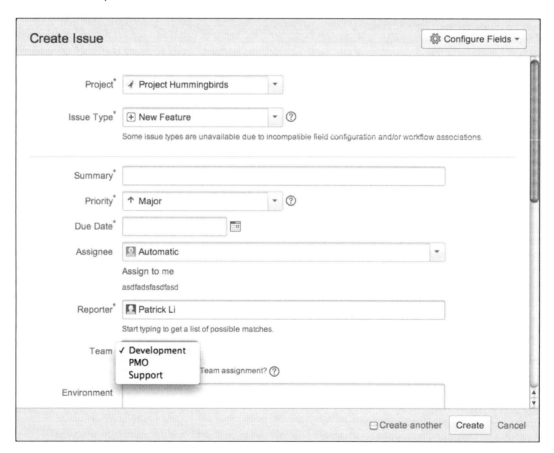

How it works...

In our script, we use jQuery to select the **Team** custom field based on its element ID and remove the option with value -1 (which is the **None** option) with the selector `#customfield_10103 option[value="-1"]`.

We use the **Atlassian JavaScript** (**AJS**) namespace (`AJS.$`), which is the recommended way to use jQuery in JIRA.

Creating custom field with custom logic

All custom fields that come out of the box with JIRA have predefined purposes, such as text field, which allows users to type in some simple text. It will often be useful to have a specialized custom field that does exactly what you need. Unfortunately, this often requires custom development efforts.

However, there is an add-on that provides a custom field type that lets you use Groovy scripts to power its logic.

In this recipe, we will look at how to create a custom field that uses a Groovy script to display the total number of comments on any given issue.

Getting ready

For this recipe, we need to have the Script Runner add-on installed. You can download it from the following link or install it directly from the Universal Plugin Manager at `https://marketplace.atlassian.com/plugins/com.onresolve.jira.groovy.groovyrunner`.

You may also want to get familiar with Groovy scripting at `http://groovy.codehaus.org`.

How to do it...

Creating a scripted field is a two-step process. We first need to create an instance of the custom field in JIRA and then add the script to it:

1. Log in to JIRA as a JIRA administrator.
2. Navigate to **Administration | Issues | Field Configurations**.
3. Click on the **Add Custom Field** button and select **Advanced** from the dialog box.

4. Scroll down and select **Scripted Field** from the list, and click on **Next**, as shown in the following screenshot:

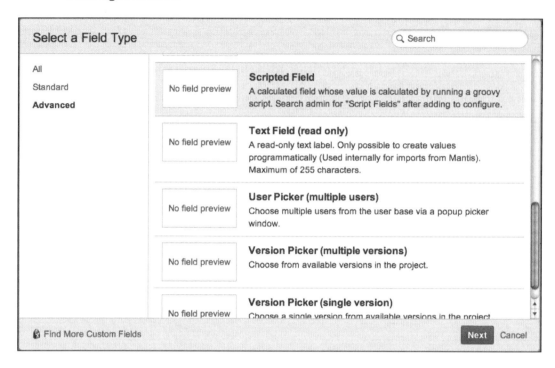

5. Name our new custom field `Total Comments`, and add it to the appropriate screens.

6. Navigate to **Add-ons | Script Fields**.

7. Click on the **Edit** link for the **Total Comments** field.

8. Enter the following Groovy script in the script text box:

```
import com.atlassian.jira.ComponentManager

def commentManager = ComponentManager.getInstance().
getCommentManager()

def numberOfComments = commentManager.getComments(issue).size()

return numberOfComments ? numberOfComments as Double : null
```

9. Select **Number Field** for **Script Template**, and click on **OK** as shown in the following screenshot:

How it works...

The scripted field type is an example of what is called **calculated** custom field type. The calculated custom field type is a special custom field that derives (calculates) its value based on some predefined logic, in this case, our Groovy script. Every time the field is displayed, JIRA will recalculate the field's value so it is always kept up to date.

3
JIRA Workflows

In this chapter, we will cover:

- ▶ Creating a new workflow
- ▶ Adding screens to workflow transitions
- ▶ Using common transitions
- ▶ Using global transitions
- ▶ Restricting the availability of workflow transitions
- ▶ Validating user input in workflow transitions
- ▶ Performing additional processing after a transition is executed
- ▶ Rearranging the workflow transition bar
- ▶ Restricting the resolution values in a transition
- ▶ Preventing issue updates in selected statuses
- ▶ Making a field required during workflow transition
- ▶ Creating custom workflow transition logic
- ▶ Sharing workflows with workflow bundles

Introduction

Workflows are one of the core and most powerful features in JIRA. They control how issues in JIRA move from one stage to another as they are being worked on, often passing from one assignee to another. For this reason, workflows can be thought of as the life cycle of issues.

Unlike many other systems, JIRA allows you to create your own workflows to resemble the work processes you may already have in your organization. This is a good example of how JIRA is able to adapt to your needs without having you change the way you work.

In this chapter, we will learn about not only how to create workflows with the new workflow designer, but also how to use workflow components, such as conditions and validators, to add additional behavior to your workflows. We will also look at the many different add-ons that are available to expand the possibilities of what you can do with workflows.

Creating a new workflow

A workflow is like a flowchart, in which issues can go from one state to another by following the direction paths between the states. In JIRA's workflow terminology, the states are called **statuses**, and the paths are called **transitions**; we will use these two major components when creating a workflow.

In this recipe, we will create a new, simple workflow from scratch. We will look at how to use existing statuses, create new statuses, and link them together using transitions.

How to do it...

The first step is to create a new skeleton workflow in JIRA:

1. Log in to JIRA as a JIRA administrator.
2. Navigate to **Administration | Issues | Workflows**.
3. Click on the **Add Workflow** button and name the workflow Simple Workflow.
4. Click on the **Diagram** button to use the workflow designer, or diagram mode.

The following screenshot explains some of the key elements of the workflow designer:

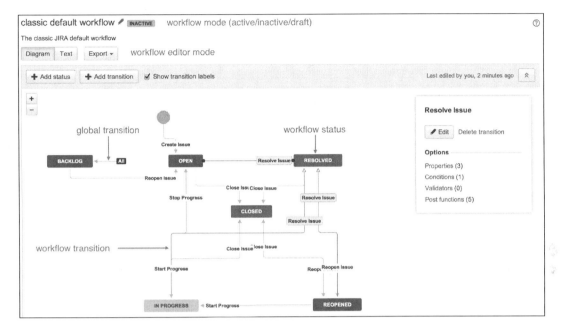

As of now, we have created a new, inactive workflow. The next step is to add various statuses for the issues to go through. JIRA comes with a number of existing statuses such as **In Progress** and **Resolved** for us to use:

1. Click on the **Add existing status** button.
2. Select the **In Progress** status from the list and click on **Add**.

3. Repeat the steps to add the **Closed** status:

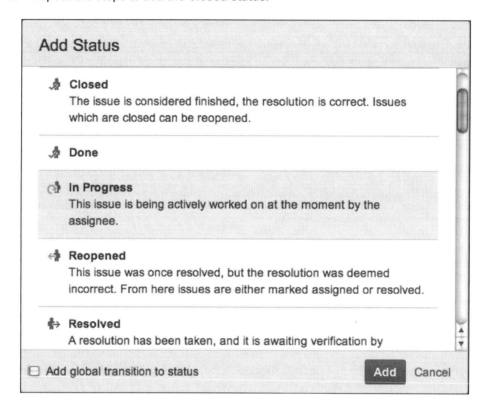

Once you have added the statuses to the workflow, you can drag them around to reposition them on the canvas. We can also create new statuses as follows:

1. Click on the **Create new status** button.
2. Name the new status Backlog and click on **Create**.

Now that we have added the statuses, we need to link them using transitions:

1. Select the originating status, which in this example is **Open**.

2. Click on the small circle around the **Open** status and drag your cursor onto the **In Progress** status. This will prompt you to provide details for the new transition as shown in the following screenshot:

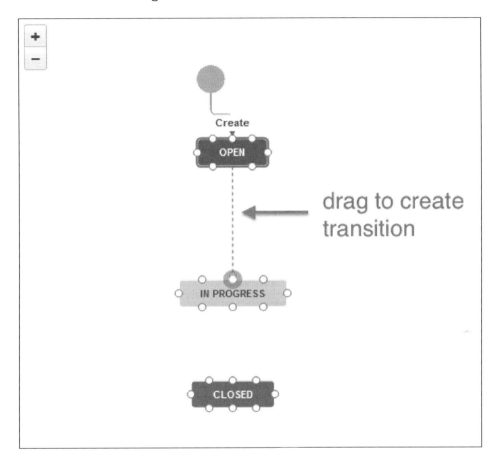

3. Name the new transition Start Progress and select the **None** option for the **Transition** screen.

4. Repeat the steps to create a transition called **Close** between the **In Progress** and **Closed** statuses.

You should finish with a workflow that looks like the following screenshot:

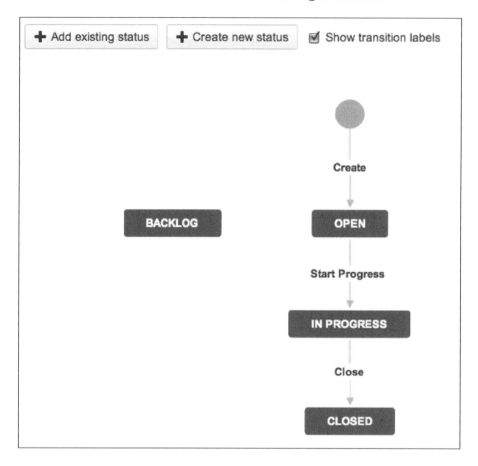

At this point, the workflow is inactive, which means it is not being used by a project and you can edit it without any restrictions. Workflows are applied on a project and issue type basis. Perform the following steps to apply the new workflow to a project:

1. Select the project to apply the workflow to.
2. Click on the **Administration** tab to go to the project administration page.
3. Select **Workflows** from the left-hand side of the page.
4. Click on **Add Existing** from the **Add Workflow** menu.
5. Select the new **Simple Workflow** from the dialog and click on **Next**.
6. Choose the issue types to apply the workflow to and click on **Finish**.

After we have applied the workflow to a project, the workflow is placed in the active state. So, if we now create a new issue in the target project of the selected issue type, our new **Simple Workflow** will be used.

Adding screens to workflow transitions

When users execute a workflow transition, we have an option to display an intermediate workflow screen. This is a very useful way to collect some additional information from the user. For example, the default JIRA workflow will display a screen for users to select the **Resolution** value when the issue is resolved.

 Issues with resolution values are considered completed. You should only add the **Resolution** field to workflow screens that represent the closing of an issue.

Getting ready

We need to have a workflow to configure, such as the **Simple Workflow** that was created in the previous recipe. We also need to have screens to display; JIRA's out-of-the-box **Workflow Screen** and **Resolve Issue Screen** will suffice, but if you have created your own screens, they can also be used.

How to do it...

Perform the following steps to add a screen to a workflow transition:

1. Select the workflow to update, such as our **Simple Workflow**.
2. Click on the **Edit** button if the workflow is active. This will create a draft workflow for us to work on.
3. Select the **Start Progress** transition and click on the **Edit** link from the panel on the right-hand side.
4. Select **Workflow Screen** from the **Transition** screen dropdown and click on **Save**.
5. Repeat steps 3 and 4 to add **Resolve Issue Screen** to the **Close** transition.

If we are working with a draft workflow, we must click on the **Publish Draft** button to apply our changes to the live workflow.

 If you do not see your changes reflected, it is most likely you forgot to publish your draft workflow.

Using common transitions

Often, you will have transitions that need to be made available from several different statuses in a workflow, such as the **Resolve** and **Close** transitions. In other words, these are transitions that have a common destination status but many different originating statuses.

To help you simplify the process of creating these transitions, JIRA lets you reuse an existing transition as a common transition if it has the same destination status.

[**Common transitions** are transitions that have the same destination status but different originating statuses.]

A common transition has an additional advantage of ensuring that transition screens and other relevant configurations, such as validators, will stay consistent. Otherwise, you will have to constantly check the various transitions every time you make a change to one of them.

How to do it...

Perform the following steps to create and use common transitions in your workflow:

1. Select the **Simple Workflow** and click on the **Edit** link to create a draft.
2. Select the **Diagram** mode.
3. Create a transition between two steps, for example, Open and Closed.
4. Create another transition from a different step to the same destination step and click on the **Reuse a transition** tab:

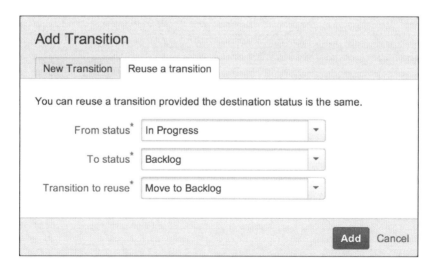

5. Select the transition created in step 3 from the **Transition to reuse** dropdown, and click on **Add**.

6. Click on **Publish Draft** to apply the change.

If you are running JIRA prior to JIRA 6.2, you should know that a common transition is only supported in the classic diagram mode of the workflow editor. So, what you need to do here is enter the **Diagram** mode and then click on the **Enter classic mode** option. When you create new transitions, you can select the **Use Common Transition** option as shown in the following screenshot:

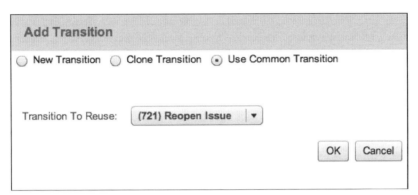

See also

Refer to the *Using global transitions* recipe.

Using global transitions

While a common transition is a great way to *share* transitions in a workflow and reduce the amount of management work that will otherwise be required, it has the following two limitations:

> ▶ Currently, it is only supported in the classic diagram mode (if running on older JIRA versions)

> ▶ You still have to manually create the transitions between the various steps

As your workflow starts to become complicated, explicitly creating the transitions becomes a tedious job; this is where **global transitions** come in.

A global transition is similar to a common transition in the sense that they both share the property of having a single destination status. The difference between the two is that the global transition is a single transition that is available to all the statuses in a workflow.

In this recipe, we will look at how to use global transitions so that issues can be transitioned to the **Backlog** status throughout the workflow.

Getting ready

As usual, you need to have a workflow you can edit. Since we will demonstrate how global transitions work, you need to have a status called **Backlog** in your workflow and ensure that there are no transitions linked to it.

How to do it...

Perform the following steps to create and use global transitions in your workflow:

1. Select and edit the workflow you will be adding the global transition to.
2. Select the **Diagram** mode.
3. Select the **Backlog** status.
4. Check the **Allow all statuses to transition to this one** option.
5. Click on **Publish Draft** to apply the change.

The following screenshot depicts the preceding steps:

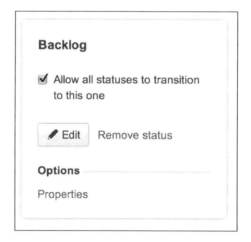

If you are running JIRA prior to JIRA 6.2, you need to click on the **Add a global transition** button and then specify the transition name and screen, as shown in the following screenshot:

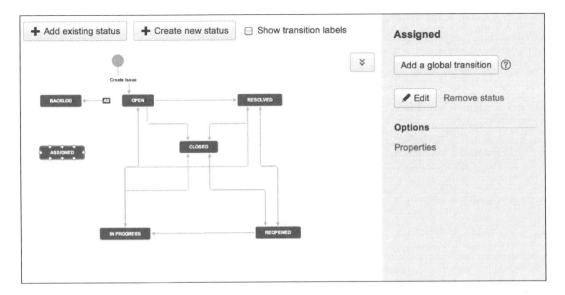

 You can only add global transitions in the **Diagram** mode.

After the global transition is added to the **Backlog** status, you will be able to transition issues to **Backlog** regardless of its current status.

See also

Refer to the following recipe, *Restricting the availability of workflow transitions*, on how to remove a transition when an issue is already in the **Backlog** status.

Restricting the availability of workflow transitions

Workflow transitions, by default, are accessible to anyone who has access to the issue. There will be times when you would want to restrict access to certain transitions. For example, you might want to restrict access to the **Move to Backlog** transition for the following reasons:

- The transition should only be available to users in specific groups or project roles
- Since the transition is a global transition, it is available to all the workflow statuses, but it does not make sense to show the transition when the issue is already in the **Backlog** status

To restrict the availability of a workflow transition, we can use workflow conditions.

Getting ready

For this recipe, we need to have the JIRA Suite Utilities add-on installed. You can download it from the following link or install it directly from the Universal Plugin Manager:

```
https://marketplace.atlassian.com/plugins/com.googlecode.jira-suite-
utilities
```

How to do it...

We need to create a new custom field configuration scheme in order to set up a new set of select list options:

1. Select and edit the workflow to configure.
2. Select the **Diagram** mode.
3. Click on the **Move to Backlog** global workflow transition.
4. Click on the **Conditions** link from the panel towards the right-hand side.
5. Click on **Add condition**, select the **Value Field** condition (provided by JIRA Suite Utilities) from the list, and click on **Add**.
6. Select the **Status** field for **Field**, != for **Condition**, **Backlog** for **Value**, and **String** for **Comparison Type**.
7. Click on the **Add** button to complete the condition setup.
8. Click on the **Add** condition again and select **User** in the **Project Role** condition.
9. Select the **Developer** project role and click on **Add**.
10. Click on **Publish Draft** to apply the change.

Refer to the following screenshot:

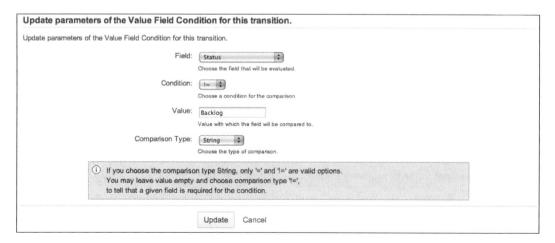

After you have applied the workflow conditions, the transition **Move to Backlog** will no longer be available if the issue is already in the **Backlog** status and/or the current user is not in the **Developer** project role.

There's more...

Using the **Value Field** condition (that comes with the JIRA Suite Utilities add-on) is one of the many ways in which we can restrict the availability of a transition based on the issue's previous status. There is another add-on called **JIRA Misc Workflow Extensions**, which comes with a **Previous Status** condition for this very use case. You can download it from `https://marketplace.atlassian.com/plugins/com.innovalog.jmwe.jira-misc-workflow-extensions`.

When you have more than one workflow condition applied to the transition, as in our example, the default behavior is that all conditions must pass for the transition to be available.

You can change this so that only one condition needs to pass for the transition to be available by changing the condition group logic from **All of the following conditions** to **Any of the following conditions**, as shown in the following screenshot:

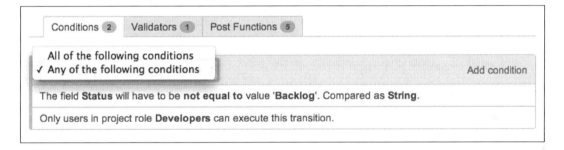

Validating user input in workflow transitions

For workflow transitions that have transition screens, you can add validation logic to make sure what the users put in is what you are expecting. This is a great way to ensure data integrity, and we can do this with workflow validators.

In this recipe, we will add a validator to perform a date comparison between a custom field and the issue's create date, so the date value we select for the custom field must be after the issue's create date.

Getting ready

For this recipe, we need to have the JIRA Suite Utilities add-on installed. You can download it from the following link or install it directly using the Universal Plugin Manager:

```
https://marketplace.atlassian.com/plugins/com.googlecode.jira-suite-
utilities
```

Since we are also doing a date comparison, we need to create a new date custom field called `Start Date` and add it to the **Workflow Screen**.

How to do it...

Perform the following steps to add validation rules during a workflow transition:

1. Select and edit the workflow to configure.

2. Select the **Diagram** mode.

3. Select the **Start Progress** transition and click on the **Validators** link towards the right-hand side.

4. Click on the **Add validator** link and select **Date Compare** from the list.

5. Select the **Start Date** custom field for **This date**, **>** for **Condition**, and **Created** for **Compare with**, and click on **Update** to add the validator:

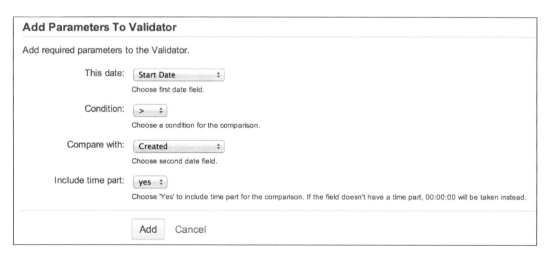

6. Click on **Publish Draft** to apply the change.

After we add the validator, if we now try to select a date that is before the issue's create date, JIRA will prompt you with an error message and stop the transition from going through, as shown in the following screenshot:

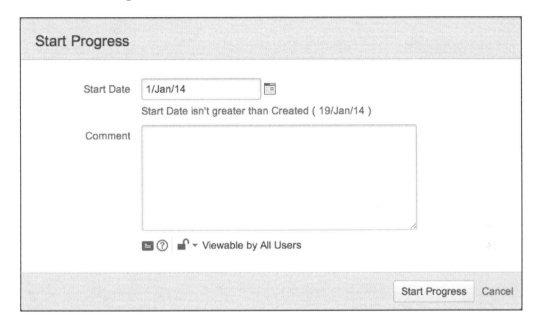

How it works...

Validators are run after the user has executed the transition but before the transition starts. This way, validators can intercept and prevent a transition from going through if one or more of the validation logics fail.

 If you have more than one validator, all of them must pass for the transition to go through.

See also

Validators can be used to make a field required only during workflow transitions. Refer to the *Making a field required during workflow transition* recipe for more details.

Performing additional processing after a transition is executed

JIRA allows you to perform additional tasks as part of a workflow transition through the use of post functions. JIRA makes heavy use of post functions internally, for example, with the out-of-the-box workflow, when you reopen an issue, the resolution field value is cleared automatically.

In this recipe, we will look at how to add post functions to a workflow transition. We will add a post function to automatically clear out the value stored in the **Reason for Backlog** custom field when we take it out of the **Backlog** status.

Getting ready

By default, JIRA comes with a post function that can change the values for standard issue fields, but since **Reason for Backlog** is a custom field, we need to have the JIRA Suite Utilities add-on installed.

You can download it from the following link or install it directly using the Universal Plugin Manager:

```
https://marketplace.atlassian.com/plugins/com.googlecode.jira-suite-
utilities
```

How to do it...

We need to create a new custom field configuration scheme in order to set up a new set of select list options:

1. Select and edit the workflow to configure.
2. Select the **Diagram** mode.
3. Click on the **Move to Backlog** global workflow transition.
4. Click on the **Post functions** link towards the right-hand side.
5. Click on **Add post function**, select **Clear Field Value post function** from the list, and click on **Add**.
6. Select the **Reason for Backlog** field from **Field** and click on the **Add** button.
7. Click on **Publish Draft** to apply the change.

With the post function in place, after you have executed the transition, the **Reason for Backlog** field will be cleared out. You can also see from the issue's change history as a part of the transition execution that where the **Status** field is changed from **Backlog** to **Open**, the change for the **Reason for Backlog** field is also recorded.

How it works...

Post functions are run after the transition has been executed. When you add a new post function, you might have noticed that the transition already has a number of post functions pre-added; this is shown in the screenshot that follows.

These post functions are system post functions that carry out important internal functions, such as keeping the search index up to date. The order of these post functions is important. For example, any changes to issue field values, such as the one we just added, should always happen before the **Re-index** post function, so by the time the transition is completed, all the field indexes are up to date and ready to be searched.

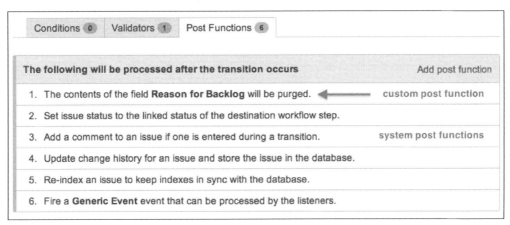

 Always add your own post functions at the top of the list.

Rearranging the workflow transition bar

By default, workflow transitions are displayed based on the order in which they are defined in the workflow (as listed in the **Text** mode), where the first two transitions will be shown as buttons and the remaining transitions will be added to the **Workflow** menu.

This sequence is determined by the order in which the transitions are added, so you cannot change that. But you can rearrange them by using the `opsbar-sequence` property.

In this recipe, we will move the **Move to Backlog** transition out from the **Workflow** menu and to its own transition button so that the users can easily access it.

How to do it...

Perform the following steps to rearrange the order of transitions to be displayed in the issue transition bar:

1. Select and edit the workflow to configure.
2. Select the **Move to Backlog** transition.
3. Click on the **View Properties** button.
4. Enter `opsbar-sequence` for **Property Name** and the value `30` in **Property Value** and click on **Add**.
5. Click on **Publish Draft** to apply the change:

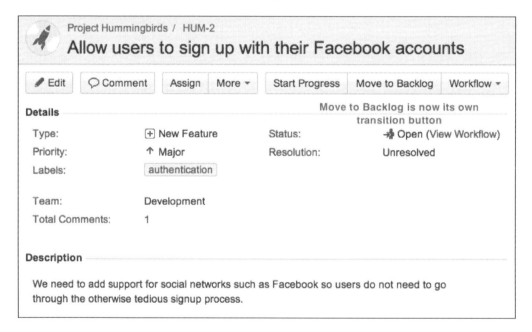

How it works...

The `opsbar-sequence` property orders the workflow transitions numerically, from smallest to largest. Its value needs to be a positive integer. The smaller the number, the further at the front the transition will appear.

There's more...

JIRA only displays the first two transitions as buttons. You can change this setting by editing the `ops.bar.group.size.opsbar-transitions` property in the `jira-config.properties` file located in your `JIRA_HOME` directory.

All you have to do is edit the file, set the property to the desired number of transition buttons to display as shown (we are setting the number of transition buttons to 3), and restart JIRA:

```
ops.bar.group.size.opsbar-transitions=3
```

As depicted in the following screenshot, JIRA now shows three transition buttons instead of two:

 If you do not see the `jira-config.properties` file, you can simply create a new file with the same name and add your properties there.

Restricting the resolution values in a transition

Normally, issue resolution values such as **Fixed** and **Won't Fix** are global, so regardless of the project and issue type, the same set of values will be available. As you implement different workflows in JIRA, you may find that certain resolutions are not relevant in a given workflow.

In this recipe, we will select a subset of the global resolutions available when we close issues using our **Simple Workflow**.

How to do it...

Perform the following steps to selectively include a subset of resolutions for a given workflow transition:

1. Select and edit the **Simple Workflow**.
2. Select the **Close** workflow transition.
3. Click on the **View Properties** button.

4. Enter `jira.field.resolution.include` for **Property Name** and the IDs (comma separated) for resolutions we want to make available into **Property Value**. So, if we want to include the resolutions **Fixed, Won't Fix**, and **Duplicate**, we need to specify values 1, 2, and 3 as the property values.

5. Click on **Publish Draft** to apply the change.

There's more...

Other than selecting a subset of resolutions, there is also a `jira.field.resolution.exclude` property that lets you exclude a subset of resolutions from the global list.

Preventing issue updates in selected statuses

By default, when an issue is in the **Closed** status, it cannot be updated. It is a good practice to make issues read-only when they are in a status that signifies logical completion.

In this recipe, we will make sure that when an issue is moved to the **Backlog** status, it can no longer be updated until it is moved back to the **Open** status.

How to do it...

Perform the following steps to make an issue read-only when it is in the **Backlog** status:

1. Select and edit the **Simple Workflow**.

2. Select the **Backlog** workflow step.

3. Click on the **Properties** link from the panel on the right-hand side.

4. Enter `jira.issue.editable` for **Property Name** and the value `false` into **Property Value** and click on **Add**.

5. Click on **Publish Draft** to apply the change.

Making a field required during workflow transition

Using field configuration to make a field required will make the field required all the time. There are many use cases where you will only need the field to be required during certain workflow transitions.

Getting ready

For this recipe, we need to have the JIRA Suite Utilities add-on installed. You can download it from the following link or install it directly using the Universal Plugin Manager:

```
https://marketplace.atlassian.com/plugins/com.googlecode.jira-suite-
utilities
```

How to do it...

Perform the following steps to make the **Reason for Backlog** field required during the **Move to Backlog** transition:

1. Select and edit the **Simple Workflow**.
2. Select the **Diagram** mode.
3. Click on the **Move to Backlog** global workflow transition.
4. Click on the **Validators** link from the panel on the right-hand side.
5. Click on **Add validator**, select the **Fields Required** validator from the list, and click on **Add**.
6. Select the **Reason for Backlog** field from **Available fields** and click on **Add >>**. This will add the selected field to the **Required fields** list:

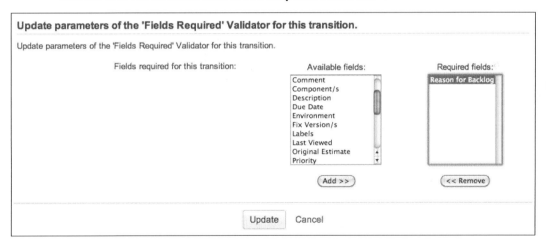

7. Click on the **Add** button to complete the validator setup.
8. Click on **Publish Draft** to apply the change.

After you have added the validator, if you try to execute the **Move to Backlog** transition without specifying a value for the **Reason for Backlog** field, JIRA will prompt you with an error message as shown in the following screenshot:

Creating custom workflow transition logic

In previous recipes, we have looked at using workflow conditions, validators, and post functions that come out of the box with JIRA and from other third-party add-ons.

In this recipe, we will take a look at how to use scripts to define our own validation rules for a workflow validator. We will address a common use case, which is to make a field required during a workflow transition only when another field is set to a certain value.

So, our validation logic will be as follows:

▶ If the **Resolution** field is set to **Fixed**, the **Solution Details** field will be required

▶ If the **Resolution** field is set to a value other than **Fixed**, the **Solution Details** field will not be required

Getting ready

For this recipe, we need to have the Script Runner add-on installed. You can download it from the following link or install it directly using the Universal Plugin Manager:

```
https://marketplace.atlassian.com/plugins/com.onresolve.jira.groovy.
groovyrunner
```

You might also want to get familiar with Groovy scripting (`http://groovy.codehaus.org`).

How to do it...

Perform the following steps to set up a validator with custom-scripted logic:

1. Select and edit the **Simple Workflow**.
2. Select the **Diagram** mode.
3. Click on the **Move to Backlog** global workflow transition.
4. Click on the **Validators** link from the panel on the right-hand side.
5. Click on **Add validator**, select **Script Validator** from the list, and click on **Add**. Now enter the following script code in the **Condition** textbox:

```
import com.opensymphony.workflow.InvalidInputException
import com.atlassian.jira.ComponentManager
import org.apache.commons.lang.StringUtils

def customFieldManager =
  ComponentManager.getInstance().getCustomFieldManager()
def solutionField =
  customFieldManager.getCustomFieldObjectByName("Solution
  Details")

def resolution = issue.getResolutionObject().getName()
def solution = issue.getCustomFieldValue(solutionField)

if(resolution == "Fixed" && StringUtils.isBlank(solution))
{
    false
} else {
    true
}
```

6. Enter the text `"You must provide the Solution Details if the Resolution is set to Fixed."` in the **Error** field.
7. Select **Solution Details** for **Field**.
8. Click on the **Add** button to complete the validator setup.
9. Click on **Publish Draft** to apply the change.

Your validator configuration should look something like the following screenshot:

Once we add our custom validator, every time the **Move to Backlog** transition is executed, the Groovy script will run. If the resolution field is set to **Fixed** and the **Solution Details** field is empty, we will get a message from the **Error** field as shown in the following screenshot:

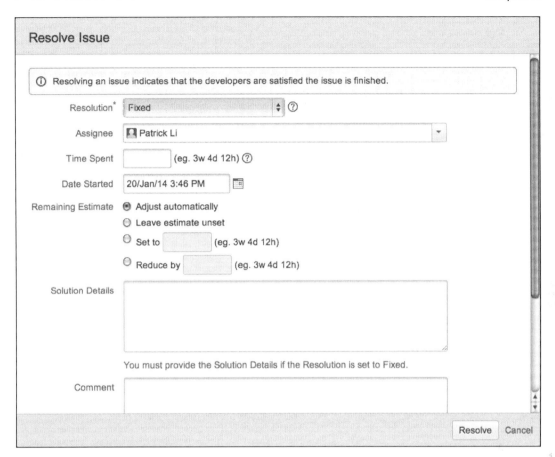

How it works...

The Script Validator works just like any other validator, except that we can define our own validation logic using Groovy scripts. So, let's go through the script and see what it does.

We first get the **Solution Details** custom field via its name, as shown in the following line of code. If you have more than one custom field with the same name, you need to use its ID instead of its name.

```
def solutionField =
   customFieldManager.getCustomFieldObjectByName("Solution
   Details")
```

We then select the resolution value and obtain the value entered for **Solution Details** during the transition, as follows:

```
def resolution = issue.getResolutionObject().getName()
def solution = issue.getCustomFieldValue(solutionField)
```

In our example, we check the resolution name; we can also check the ID of the resolution by changing `getName()` to `getId()`.

 If you have multiple custom fields with the same name, use `getId()`.

Lastly, we check whether the **Resolution** value is **Fixed** and the **Solution Details** value is blank; in this case, we return a value of `false`, so the validation fails. All other cases will return the value `true`, so the validation passes. We also use `StringUtils.isBlank(solution)` to check for blank values so that we can catch cases when users enter empty spaces for the **Solution Details** field.

There's more...

You are not limited to creating scripted validators. With the Script Runner add-on, you can create scripted conditions and post functions using Groovy scripts.

Sharing workflows with workflow bundles

A workflow is a very complicated component in JIRA as it makes use of other components, such as custom fields and screens. JIRA is used to provide a way for you to export your workflows into XML, but due to the difference between systems, it is often very difficult to import workflows into another system.

Since JIRA 5, there is a new concept called **workflow bundle**, which makes it possible for people to share their workflows with others. With workflow bundles, it is much easier to export and import workflows from one JIRA to another. So, we will take a look at how to create a workflow bundle based on one of our own workflows.

Getting ready

For this recipe, we need to have the JIRA Workflow Sharing add-on installed. This add-on comes bundled with JIRA, but if you do not have it installed, you can download it from the following link or install it directly using the Universal Plugin Manager:

```
https://marketplace.atlassian.com/plugins/com.atlassian.jira.plugins.
jira-workflow-sharing-plugin
```

How to do it...

Perform the following steps to export an existing workflow as a workflow bundle:

1. Navigate to **Administration | Issues | Workflows**.
2. Select the workflow you want to export.
3. Select the **As Workflow** option from the **Export** drop-down menu.
4. Click on **Next**.
5. Review and update the special instructions. JIRA will autogenerate these instructions based on the add-ons used and the components that are stripped away from the workflow.
6. Click on **Export** to create the workflow bundle.

Once the workflow bundle is created, you can import it into another JIRA instance using the following steps:

1. Navigate to **Administration | Issues | Workflows**.
2. Select the **Import Workflow** option from the **Import** menu.
3. Select the **From My Computer** option.
4. Choose the exported workflow bundle file (.jwb) and click on **Next**.
5. Give a name to the new workflow and click on **Next**.
6. Map the statuses in the workflow bundle (left-hand side column) to existing statuses in your system (right-hand side column), or you can choose to simply create the missing statuses as part of the import. Once they are mapped, click on **Next**.
7. Review the import summary and click on **Import** to start the process.

There's more...

There are many people who create custom workflows and make them available to the public. When you import workflow bundles, you can select the **From Atlassian Marketplace** option to see some of the workflows others have created and try them out.

4
User Management

In this chapter, we will cover the following topics:

- ▶ Creating a new user
- ▶ Inviting a new user to sign up
- ▶ Enabling a public user sign up
- ▶ Managing groups and group memberships
- ▶ Managing project roles
- ▶ Managing default project role memberships
- ▶ Deactivating a user
- ▶ Integrating and importing users from LDAP
- ▶ Integrating with LDAP for authentication only
- ▶ Integrating with Atlassian Crowd
- ▶ Integrating with another JIRA instance for user information
- ▶ Enabling JIRA as a user repository
- ▶ Setting up single sign-on with Crowd
- ▶ Setting up a Windows domain single sign-on

Introduction

User management is often one of the most tedious and yet important aspects of any system. It lays the foundation for many other system functions, such as security and notifications.

In this chapter, we will look at the different options to create user accounts in JIRA and also how to manage users with groups and project roles. We will also look at how to integrate JIRA with external user management systems such as LDAP for both authentication and user management. Lastly, we will also cover how to make JIRA participate in various single sign-on environments.

Creating a new user

In order to access and use JIRA, you need to be a valid user. Normally, while using the built-in JIRA user management feature, users are created and stored in the JIRA database. In this recipe, we will look at how to create new user accounts in JIRA.

How to do it...

Proceed with the following steps to create a user account in JIRA:

1. Log in to JIRA as a JIRA administrator.
2. Navigate to **Administration | User Management | Users**.
3. Click on the **Create User** button.
4. Fill in the new user details and click on **Create**.

Field	Value
Username	This is a unique identifier for the user. This is what the user will use to log in to JIRA. You can use formats such as `firstname.lastname` or the user e-mail to ensure uniqueness.
	Since JIRA 6, the username can be changed after it is set.
Password	This is the password for the user to authenticate. You need to leave this blank for JIRA to generate a random password.
Confirm	This is to repeat the password.
Full Name	This is the full name of the user.
Email	This is the e-mail address of the user.
Send Notification Email	This sends an e-mail to the user (based on the **Email** field) with a link to reset their password.
	This requires JIRA to have an outgoing mail server setup.

The previous fields in the table will create a normal user account. By default, the user will be added to the *jira-users* group. If you have set up other groups for the *JIRA Users* global permission, then the new user will be added to those groups. The following screenshot shows a normal user account:

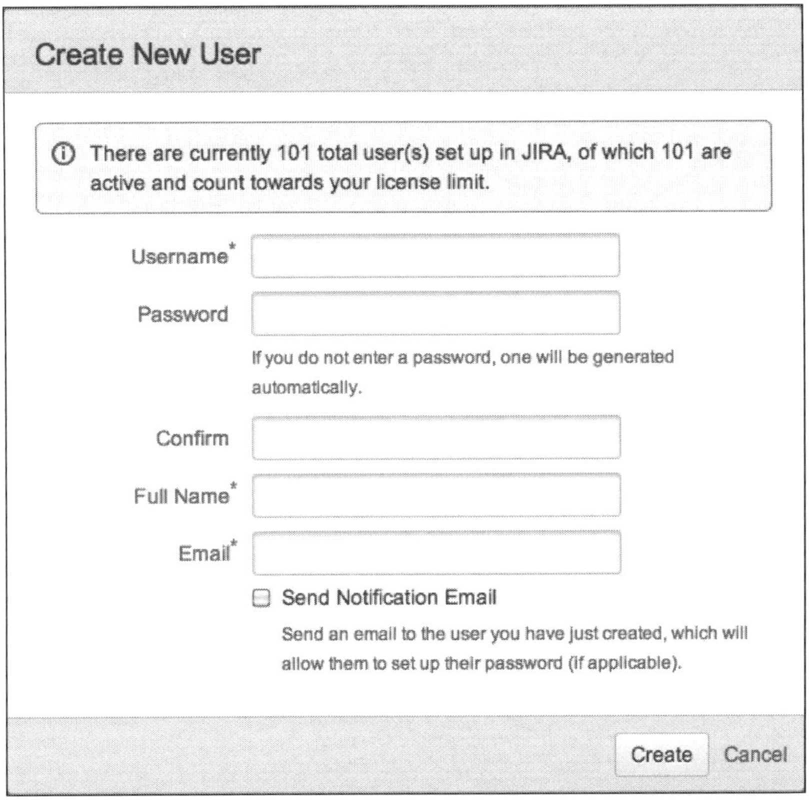

Create New User

(i) There are currently 101 total user(s) set up in JIRA, of which 101 are active and count towards your license limit.

Username*

Password

If you do not enter a password, one will be generated automatically.

Confirm

Full Name*

Email*

☐ Send Notification Email

Send an email to the user you have just created, which will allow them to set up their password (if applicable).

Create   Cancel

Inviting a new user to sign up

In the previous recipe, *Creating a new user*, we looked at how JIRA administrators can manually create a new user account. This process requires the administrator to fill in all the user information, including the username and password. Another option is to invite the users to sign up and create their accounts on their own.

Getting ready

Since we will be sending out invitation e-mails to users, we need to make sure JIRA has been configured with an outgoing mail server. We also need to have a valid e-mail address for each of the users we want to invite. When the user signs up with the invitation, the account will be created with the same e-mail.

How to do it...

Proceed with the following steps to invite users to sign up and create their own accounts:

1. Navigate to **Administration | User Management | Users**.
2. Click on the **Invite Users** button.
3. Enter the e-mail addresses for people you want to invite. You can invite more than one person by entering multiple e-mail addresses separated by a comma.
4. Click on the **Send** button to send out invitation e-mails, as shown in the following screenshot:

How it works...

JIRA will send out an invitation e-mail to each invited user, which is similar to the one shown in the following screenshot. The e-mail will contain the **Sign Up** link, which will expire after seven days. If the invited user has not signed up within the time period, a new invitation needs to be sent.

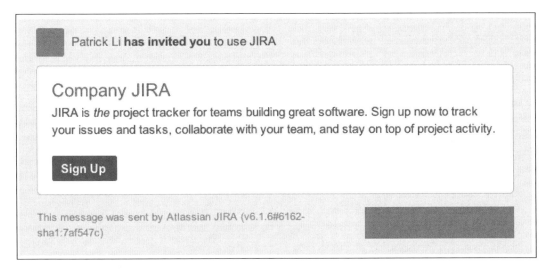

Enabling a public user sign up

In the previous recipes, we looked at how to manually create new user accounts and invite users to create new accounts. These are the two options JIRA administrators have when your JIRA instance is used internally.

However, if your JIRA is set up to be used by the public, such as a support system, you would want to let your customers to freely sign up for a new account, rather than having them to wait for the administrator to manually create each account.

How to do it...

Proceed with the following steps to enable a public user sign up:

1. Navigate to **Administration | System | General Configuration**.
2. Click on the **Edit Settings** button.
3. Set the **Mode** option to **Public** and click on **Update**.

How it works...

JIRA can operate in two modes, public and private. In the private mode, only the administrator can create new user accounts; for example, you can use the private mode for JIRA instances that are used by internal engineering teams to track their projects, as shown in the following screenshot.

The public mode allows anyone to sign up for new accounts. The new accounts created will have normal user permissions (JIRA Users global permission), so they will be able to start using JIRA immediately.

Welcome to Your Company JIRA

Username [   ]

Password [   ]

☐ Remember my login on this computer

Not a member? Sign up for an account.

[Log In] Can't access your account?

There's more...

To help prevent spammers, JIRA comes with the CAPTCHA challenge-response feature to make sure there is a real person signing up for a new account and not an automated bot. To enable the CAPTCHA feature, proceed with the following steps:

1. Navigate to **Administration | System | General Configuration**.
2. Click on the **Edit Settings** button.
3. Set the **CAPTCHA on signup** option to **On** and click on **Update**.

Once you have enabled CAPTCHA, the **Sign up** form will include a string of randomly generated alphanumeric characters that must be typed in correctly for a new account to be generated, as shown in the following screenshot:

Sign up

Full Name[*] [   ]

Email[*] [   ]

Username[*] [   ]

Password[*] [   ]

Confirm Password[*] [   ]

Please enter the word as shown below

[   ]

oilaged ↻

[Sign up] Cancel

Managing groups and group membership

Groups are a common way of managing users in any information system. While groups are usually based on positions and responsibilities within an organization, it is important to note that groups simply represent a collection of users. In JIRA, groups provide an effective way to apply configuration settings to users, such as permissions and notifications.

Groups are global in JIRA—this means if you belong to the *jira-administrators* group, you will always be in that group regardless of the project you are accessing.

In this recipe, we will look at how to create a new group and add users to it.

How to do it...

Proceed with the following steps to create a new group:

1. Navigate to **Administration | User Management | Groups**.
2. Enter the new group's name under the **Add Group** section.
3. Click on the **Add Group** button.

Proceed with the following steps to add users to a group:

1. Navigate to **Administration | User Management | Groups**.
2. Click on the **Edit Members** link for the group you want to manage.
3. Type in the usernames for the users you want to add to the group. You can click on the select user icon and use the user picker to find your users.
4. Click on the **Add selected users** button to add users to the group, as shown in the following screenshot:

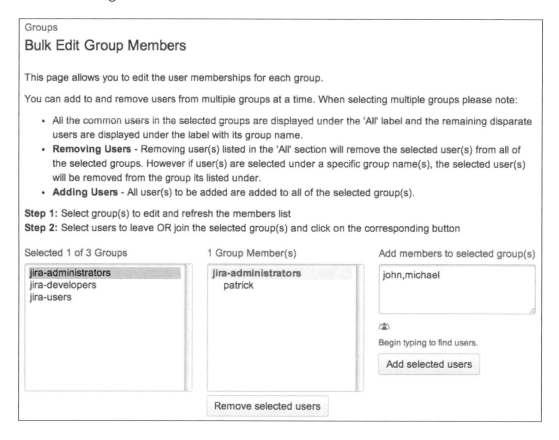

Groups

Bulk Edit Group Members

This page allows you to edit the user memberships for each group.

You can add to and remove users from multiple groups at a time. When selecting multiple groups please note:

- All the common users in the selected groups are displayed under the 'All' label and the remaining disparate users are displayed under the label with its group name.
- **Removing Users** - Removing user(s) listed in the 'All' section will remove the selected user(s) from all of the selected groups. However if user(s) are selected under a specific group name(s), the selected user(s) will be removed from the group its listed under.
- **Adding Users** - All user(s) to be added are added to all of the selected group(s).

Step 1: Select group(s) to edit and refresh the members list
Step 2: Select users to leave OR join the selected group(s) and click on the corresponding button

Selected 1 of 3 Groups | 1 Group Member(s) | Add members to selected group(s)

jira-administrators
jira-developers
jira-users

jira-administrators
    patrick

john,michael

Begin typing to find users.

Add selected users

Remove selected users

There's more...

By editing the group's membership directly, you can add and remove multiple users to and from a group in one go. However, sometimes you only need to update a single user's group membership; in these cases, you might find it easier to manage this edit option via the user's group membership interface. Proceed with the following steps to edit user groups:

1. Navigate to **Administration | User Management | Users**.

2. Click on the **Groups** link for the user you want to manage.

3. Select the group you want to join. You can choose multiple groups by holding down the *Shift* or *Ctrl* key while selecting.

4. Click on the **Join selected groups** button to add users to the group as shown in the following screenshot:

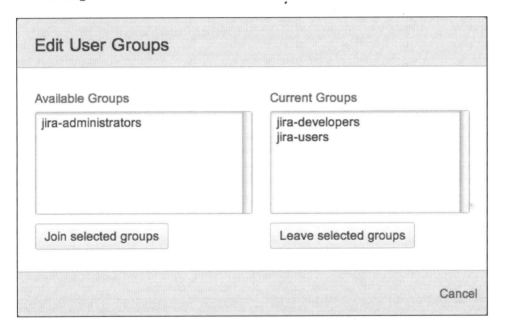

Managing project roles

In the previous chapters, we have looked at how to use groups to manage multiple users in JIRA. One limitation of using groups is that groups are global in JIRA. This means if a user is in a group, then that user is included for all projects in that group.

In real life, this is often not the case; for example, a user is a manager in a project. He/she may not be a manager in a different project. This becomes a serious problem when it comes to configuring permissions and notifications.

So, to address this limitation, JIRA provides us with **project roles**. Project roles are similar to groups; the only difference being that the membership of a project role is defined at the project level.

How to do it...

JIRA comes with three project roles out of the box: **Administrators**, **Developers**, and **Users**. So, we will first look at how to create a new project role.

Proceed with the following steps to create a new project role:

1. Navigate to **Administration | User Management | Roles**.

2. Enter the new project role's name and description.

3. Click on the **Add Project Role** button.

 Just like groups, project roles themselves are global in JIRA, but their memberships are local to each project.

Project Role Browser ⑦

You can use project roles to associate users and/or groups with specific projects. The table below shows all the project roles that are available in JIRA. Use this screen to add, edit and delete project roles. You can also click 'View Usage' to see which projects, permission schemes and notification schemes are using project roles.

Project Role Name	Description	Operations
Administrators	A project role that represents administrators in a project	View Usage · Manage Default Members · Edit · Delete
Developers	A project role that represents developers in a project	View Usage · Manage Default Members · Edit · Delete
Users	A project role that represents users in a project	View Usage · Manage Default Members · Edit · Delete

Add Project Role

Name `Project Manager`

Description `A project role that represents the PM in a project`

[Add Project Role]

Once the project role has been created, we can start adding users and groups to the concerned role for each project. To add a new user and/or group to a project role, proceed with the following steps:

1. Navigate to the target project.

2. Click on the **Administration** tab and select **Roles**.

3. Hover over the new project role and select either **Add User** or **Add Group**.

4. Select the user and/or group and click on **Update** as shown in the following screenshot:

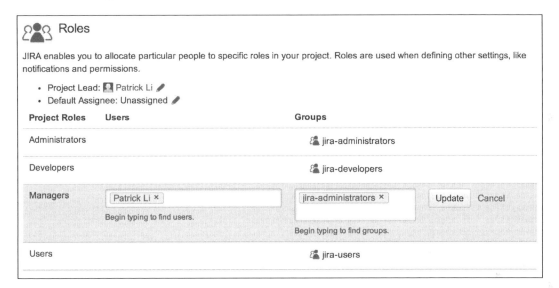

Managing default project role memberships

Project role memberships are defined per project. However, there are cases where certain users or groups need to be members of a given project role by default. In fact, JIRA has the following default members out of the box:

▸ **Administrators**: These consist of jira-administrators

▸ **Developers**: These consist of jira-developers

▸ **Users**: These consist of jira-users

With the default members, users are automatically added to the project role when a new project is created; this greatly reduces the amount of manual work required from a JIRA administrator.

How to do it...

Proceed with the following steps to define the default membership for project roles:

1. Navigate to **Administration | Issues | Roles**.
2. Click on the **Manage Default Members** link for the project role you want to configure.
3. Click on the **Edit** link of the **Default Users** column to add users to the project role.
4. Click on the **Edit** link of the **Default Groups** column to add groups to the project role, as shown in the following screenshot:

Edit Default Members for Project Role: Administrators   ⑦

The table below shows the default members (i.e. users, groups) for a project role.

NOTE: When a new project is created, it will be assigned these 'default members' for the 'Administrators' project role. Note that 'default members' apply only when a project is created. Changing the 'default members' for a project role will not affect role membership for existing projects.

• **Return to Project Role Browser**

Default Users	Default Groups
Patrick Li Edit	jira-administrators Edit

How it works...

Once you have assigned users and groups as the default members of a project role, any newly created project will have those users and groups added to the role. A good practice is to use groups for the default project role membership, as a user's role and responsibilities are likely to change over time.

It is important to note that the changes to the default membership will *not* be retrospectively applied to existing projects.

Deactivating a user

Once a user has created an issue or comment, JIRA will not allow you to delete the user. In fact, deactivating a user is usually a better approach than deleting the user completely. Once the user is deactivated, the user cannot log in to JIRA, and this will not count towards your license count.

You cannot deactivate a user when you are using external user management systems such as LDAP or Crowd from JIRA. You need to do so from the user management system of the source.

How to do it...

Proceed with the following steps to deactivate a user:

1. Navigate to **Administration | User Management | Users**.
2. Click on the **Edit** link for the user to deactivate.
3. Uncheck the **Active** option.
4. Click on the **Update** button to deactivate the user.

Deactivated users will not be able to log in to JIRA and will have the **(Inactive)** option displayed next to their name.

Integrating and importing users from LDAP

By default, JIRA manages its users and groups internally. Most organizations today often use LDAP such as Microsoft **Active Directory** (**AD**) for centralized user management, and you can integrate JIRA with LDAP. JIRA supports many different types of LDAP, including AD, OpenLDAP, and more.

There are two options to integrate JIRA with LDAP. In this recipe, we will explore the first option by using an **LDAP Connector**, and we will look at the second option in the next recipe, *Integrating with LDAP for authentication only*.

Getting ready

For this recipe, you will need to have an LDAP server up and running. You need to make sure that the JIRA server is able to access to the LDAP server and there are no glitches; for example, it is not blocked by firewalls.

At a minimum, you will also need to have the following information:

▶ The host name and port number of the LDAP server.
▶ The Base DN to search for users and groups.
▶ The credentials to access the LDAP server. If you want JIRA to be able to make changes to LDAP, make sure the credentials have write permissions.

How to do it...

Proceed with the following steps to integrate JIRA with an LDAP server:

1. Navigate to **Administration** | **User Management** | **User Directories**.
2. Click on the **Add Directory** button and select either **Microsoft Active Directory** or **LDAP** for non-AD directories.
3. Enter the LDAP server, schema, and permission settings. Refer to the following table for more details.
4. Click on the **Quick Test** button to validate JIRA's connectivity to LDAP.
5. Click on the **Save and Test** button if there are no issues connecting to LDAP.
6. Type in a username and password to run a quick test. While doing this, make sure JIRA is able to connect to LDAP, find the user and retrieve the user's group information, and lastly, is able to authenticate against LDAP.

Server Settings	Description
Name	This is an identifier for the LDAP server.
Directory type	This selects the type of the LDAP server, for example, Microsoft Active Directory. JIRA will automatically fill in the user and group schema details based on the type selected.
Hostname	This is the server where LDAP is hosted.
Port	This is the port LDAP server that is listening to incoming connections.
Use SSL	This checks whether SSL is being used on LDAP.
Username	This the user account that JIRA will use to access LDAP. This should be a dedicated account for JIRA.
Password	This is the password for the account.

LDAP Schema	Description
Base DN	This is the root node where JIRA will start the search for users and groups.
Additional User DN	This is the additional DN to further restrict a user search.
Additional Group DN	This is the additional DN to further restrict a group search.

LDAP Permission	Description
Read Only	Select this option if you do not want JIRA to make any changes to LDAP. This is the ideal option if everything, including the user's group memberships, is managed with LDAP.
Read Only, with Local Groups	This option is similar to the **Read Only** option, but lets you manage group memberships locally within JIRA. With this option, the group membership changes you make will remain in JIRA only. This is the ideal option when you only need user information from LDAP and want to manage JIRA-related groups locally.
Read/Write	Select this option if you want JIRA to be able to make direct changes to LDAP, assuming that JIRA's LDAP account has the write permission as well.

The following screenshot shows how to test the settings:

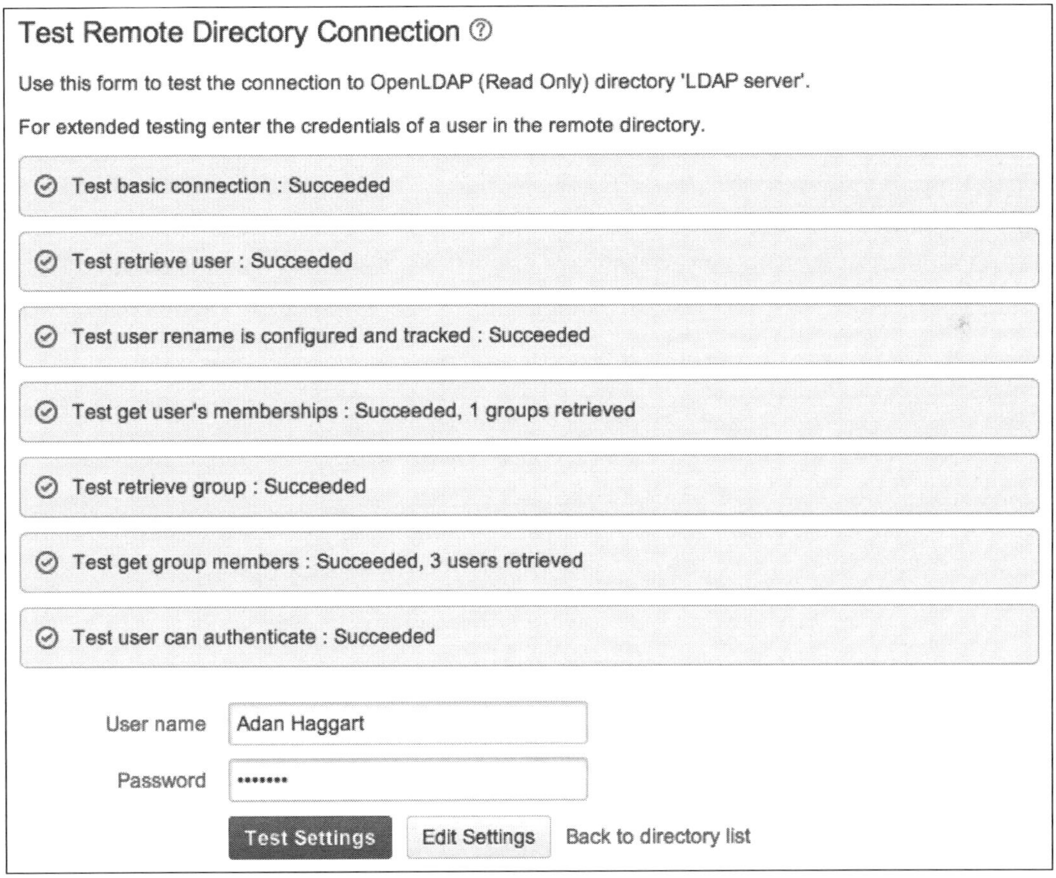

Test Remote Directory Connection ⑦

Use this form to test the connection to OpenLDAP (Read Only) directory 'LDAP server'.

For extended testing enter the credentials of a user in the remote directory.

⊘ Test basic connection : Succeeded

⊘ Test retrieve user : Succeeded

⊘ Test user rename is configured and tracked : Succeeded

⊘ Test get user's memberships : Succeeded, 1 groups retrieved

⊘ Test retrieve group : Succeeded

⊘ Test get group members : Succeeded, 3 users retrieved

⊘ Test user can authenticate : Succeeded

User name: Adan Haggart

Password: ••••••••

[Test Settings] [Edit Settings] Back to directory list

After you have added your LDAP server as a user directory, JIRA will automatically start to synchronize its user and group data. Depending on the size of your LDAP, it may take a few minutes to complete the initial synchronization. You can click on the **Back to directory list** link and see the status of the synchronization process.

Once the process is completed, you will be able to see all your LDAP users and groups show up, and you will be able to use your LDAP credentials to access JIRA.

How it works...

What we have just created in this recipe is called a **connector**. With a connector, JIRA will first pull user and group information from LDAP and create a local cache, and then periodically synchronize any deltas.

All authentication will be delegated to LDAP; so, if a user's password is updated in LDAP, it will be immediately reflected when the user attempts to log in to JIRA. It is important to note that with LDAP, users must still be in the necessary groups (for example, jira-users by default) in order to access JIRA. So, you need to make sure that you either create a group called jira-users in LDAP and add everyone to it, or grant the JIRA Users global permission to other custom groups, such as all employees.

Also note that, only users who have access to JIRA will count toward your license count.

See also

If you have a large user base in LDAP, and you only want to use LDAP for authentication, you may want to refer to the next recipe, *Integrating with LDAP for authentication only*.

Integrating with LDAP for authentication only

In the previous recipe, we have looked at how to integrate JIRA with LDAP for authentication, users, and group management. Sometimes, you might need LDAP only for authentication, and you want to keep the group membership separate from LDAP for easy management.

In this recipe, we will look at how to integrate JIRA with LDAP only for authentication.

Getting ready

Refer to the previous recipe, *Integrating and importing users from LDAP*.

How to do it...

Proceed with the following steps to integrate JIRA with an LDAP server exclusively for authentication:

1. Navigate to **Administration | User Management | User Directories**.
2. Click on the **Add Directory** button and select **Internal with LDAP Authentication**.
3. Enter the LDAP server and schema settings. Most of the parameters are identical to creating a normal LDAP connection with a few exceptions. Refer to the following table for details.
4. Click on the **Quick Test** button to validate JIRA's connectivity to LDAP.
5. Click on the **Save and Test** button if there are no issues connecting to LDAP.

Server settings	Description
Copy User on Login	This automatically copies the user from LDAP into JIRA when the user first successfully logs in to JIRA.
Default Group Membership	This automatically adds the user into the groups specified here when the user first successfully logs in to JIRA. This setting is not retrospectively applied to existing users. This is a useful feature to ensure every user who can log in to JIRA will be added to the necessary groups, such as jira-users.
Synchronize Group Memberships	This automatically copies the user's group membership to JIRA when the user successfully logs in.

How it works...

This authentication option is similar to the previous recipe with a number of key differences:

- ▶ LDAP is only used for authentication
- ▶ JIRA does not automatically synchronize the user and group information from LDAP after the initial user login
- ▶ JIRA has read-only access to LDAP
- ▶ Group membership is managed inside JIRA

With this setup, every time a user first successfully logs in to JIRA, the user is copied from LDAP to JIRA's local user repository along with the group membership (if configured to do so). Since LDAP is only used at authentication time, with no initial overhead of synchronizing all the user information, this option can provide better performance for organizations that need to synchronize a large user base in LDAP.

Integrating with Atlassian Crowd

In the previous recipe, *Integrating with LDAP for authentication only*, we looked at how to integrate JIRA to an LDAP server for user and group information. Besides using LDAP, another popular option is to use Crowd, which is available at at `https://www.atlassian.com/software/crowd/overview`.

Crowd is a user identity management solution from Atlassian, and JIRA supports Crowd integration out of the box. With Crowd, you can also set up a single sign-on option with other Crowd-enabled applications.

Getting ready

For this recipe, you will need to have a Crowd server up and running. You need to make sure that the JIRA server is able to access the Crowd server without any glitches, for example, it is not blocked by firewalls.

At a minimum, you will also need to have the following information:

▶ The Crowd server URL

▶ Credentials for the registered application in Crowd for JIRA

How to do it...

Proceed with the following steps to integrate JIRA with Crowd for user management:

1. Navigate to **Administration | User Management | User Directories**.
2. Click on the **Add Directory** button and select the **Atlassian Crowd** option.
3. Enter the Crowd server settings. Refer to the following table for details.
4. Click on the **Test Settings** button to validate JIRA's connectivity to Crowd.
5. Click on the **Save and Test** button if there are no issues connecting to Crowd.

Server Settings	Description
Name	This is an identifier for the Crowd server.
Server URL	This is the Crowd's server URL.
Application Name	This is the registered application name for JIRA inside Crowd.
Application Password	This is the password for the registered application.
Crowd Permissions	

Server Settings	Description
Read Only	Select this option if you do not want JIRA to make any changes to Crowd. This is the ideal option if everything, including the user's group membership, is managed with Crowd.
Read/Write	Select this option to let JIRA synchronize any changes back to Crowd.

Advanced Settings	Description
Enable Nested Groups	This allows groups to contain other groups as members.
Enable Incremental Synchronization	This will only synchronize deltas. Enabling this option can help improve performance.
Synchronization Interval	This determines how often (in minutes) JIRA should synchronize with Crowd for changes. Shorter intervals may cause performance issues.

See also

Refer to the *Setting up single sign-on with Crowd* recipe on how to take advantage of Crowd's single sign-on capability between JIRA and other Crowd-enabled applications.

Integrating with another JIRA instance for user information

Apart from using LDAP and Crowd, JIRA can also use another JIRA instance as a user repository. This is a good option if you have more than one JIRA instances and do not have either an LDAP or Crowd server but still want to centralize user management.

Getting ready

You need to have one JIRA setup to enable the JIRA User Server feature. Refer to the next recipe, *Enabling JIRA as a user repository*, for more details. Make sure you also review the limitations before deciding on using this option.

How to do it...

Proceed with the following steps to register a new application in JIRA:

1. Navigate to **Administration | User Management | User Directories**.
2. Click on the **Add Directory** button and select the **Atlassian JIRA** option.
3. Enter the target JIRA server settings. Most of the parameters are identical to creating a normal LDAP connection. Refer to the table from the previous recipe for details.
4. Click on the **Test Settings** button to validate connectivity.
5. Click on the **Save and Test** button if there are no issues.

See also

Refer to the next recipe, *Enabling JIRA as a user repository*, for details on how to enable your JIRA to serve other applications.

Enabling JIRA as a user repository

In the previous recipe, *Integrating with another JIRA instance for user information*, we looked at how you can use another JIRA as a user repository. In fact, you can use JIRA as a user repository for other Atlassian applications, such as Confluence.

In this recipe, we will look at how to set up JIRA so it can be used as a user repository for other systems.

How to do it...

For an application to use JIRA as a user repository, it first needs to be registered with JIRA. Proceed with the following steps to register a new application in JIRA:

1. Navigate to **Administration | User Management | JIRA User Server**.
2. Click on the **Add Application** button.
3. Enter the application name and password for the target application. This will be the credentials used by target application to access JIRA.
4. Enter the IP address of the target application. JIRA will only allow connections from the IP addresses specified here.
5. Click on the **Save** button to complete the registration, as shown in the following screenshot:

Add Application ⑦

Application name*	Confluence
	Used by application to authenticate.
Password*	••••••••••••
	Used by application to authenticate.
IP Addresses	127.0.0.1 ::1
	IP addresses, one per line.

Save   Cancel

How it works...

JIRA comes with an embedded version of Crowd, which has a subset of features of the actual product.

There are three major limitations of using JIRA as a user repository than Crowd:

- ▸ There is no single sign-on support
- ▸ The JIRA user server can handle a maximum of 500 users
- ▸ The JIRA user server can handle a maximum of five applications

Setting up single sign-on with Crowd

In previous recipes, we have looked at different options for JIRA to use external centralized user repositories, including Crowd. One of the advantages of integrating JIRA with Crowd is its single sign-on (SSO) abilities.

Web-based applications integrated with Crowd are able to participate in an SSO environment; so, when a user is logged in to one application, he/she will be automatically logged in to all other applications.

If you are looking for single sign-on in a Windows environment where users will be automatically logged on to applications with their workstation, read the next recipe, *Setting up a Windows domain single sign-on*.

Getting ready

Before you can set up SSO with Crowd, you will first need to integrate JIRA with Crowd for user management. Refer to the *Integrating with Atlassian Crowd* recipe for details.

If you have already integrated JIRA with Crowd, you will need to have the following information:

- ► The application name assigned to JIRA in Crowd
- ► The password for JIRA to access Crowd
- ► A copy of the `crowd.properties` file from the `<CROWD_INSTALL>/client/conf` directory

How to do it...

Proceed with the following steps to enable SSO with Crowd:

1. Shut down JIRA if it is running.

2. Open the `seraph-config.xml` file located in the `<JIRA_INSTALL>/atlassian-jira/WEB-INF/classes` directory in a text editor.

3. Locate the line that contains `com.atlassian.jira.security.login.JiraSeraphAuthenticator` and comment it out so it looks like the following:

   ```
   <!--
   <authenticator class="com.atlassian.jira.security.login.
   JiraSeraphAuthenticator"/>
   -->
   ```

4. Locate the line that contains `com.atlassian.jira.security.login.SSOSeraphAuthenticator` and uncomment it so it looks like the following:

   ```
   <authenticator class="com.atlassian.jira.security.login.
   SSOSeraphAuthenticator"/>
   ```

5. Copy the `crowd.properties` file to the `<JIRA_INSTALL>/atlassian-jira/WEB-INF/classes` directory.

6. Open `crowd.properties` in a text editor and update the properties listed in the following table.

7. Start up JIRA again.

Parameter	Value
`application.name`	This is the application name configured in Crowd for JIRA.
`application.password`	This the password for the application.
`application.login.url`	This is JIRA's base URL (you can get this from JIRA's General Configurations).
`crowd.base.url`	This is Crowd's base URL.
`session.validationinterval`	This is the duration (in minutes) a Crowd SSO session will remain valid. Setting this to 0 will invalidate the session immediately and will have a performance penalty. It is recommended to set this at a higher value.

Once JIRA has started up again, it will participate in SSO sessions in all Crowd SSO-enabled applications, for example, if you have multiple JIRA instances integrated to Crowd for SSO, you will only need to log in to one of the JIRAs.

 Make sure you also have a backup copy of the file before you make any changes.

Setting up a Windows domain single sign-on

If your organization is running a Windows domain, you can configure JIRA so that the users are automatically logged in when they log in to the domain with their workstations.

Getting ready

For this recipe, we will need the Kerberos SSO Authenticator for JIRA. You can get it at `http://www.appfusions.com/display/KBRSCJ/Home`.

You will also need to have the following set up:

▶ A service account in Active Directory for JIRA to use

▶ An **Service Principle Name** (**SPN**) for JIRA

How to do it...

Setting up the Windows domain SSO is not a simple task as it involves many aspects of your network configuration. It is highly recommended that you engage the product vendor to ensure smooth implementation.

Proceed with the following steps to set up the Windows domain SSO:

1. Shut down JIRA if it is running.

2. Copy `login.conf`, `krb5.conf`, and `spnego-exclusion.properties` to the `<JIRA_INSTALL>/atlassian-jira/WEB-INF/classes` directory.

3. Copy `appfusions-jira-seraph-4.0.0.jar` and `appfusions-spnego-r7_3.jar` to the `<JIRA_INSTALL>/atlassian-jira/WEB-INF/lib` directory.

4. Open the `web.xml` file located in the `<JIRA_INSTALL>/atlassian-jira/WEB-INF` directory in a text editor.

5. Add the following XML snippet before the `THIS MUST BE THE LAST FILTER IN THE DEFINED CHAIN` entry. Make sure you update the values for the following parameters:

    ❑ For `spnego.krb5.conf`, use the full path to the `spnego.krb5.conf` file

    ❑ For `spnego.login.conf`, use the full path to the `spnego.login.conf` file

    ❑ For `spnego.preauth.username`, use the username of the service account

    ❑ For `spnego.preauth.password`, use the password of the service account

```
<filter>
  <filter-name>SpnegoHttpFilter</filter-name>
  <filter-class>net.sourceforge.spnego.SpnegoHttpFilter</filter-
class>
  <init-param>
    <param-name>spnego.allow.basic</param-name>
    <param-value>true</param-value>
  </init-param>
  <init-param>
    <param-name>spnego.allow.localhost</param-name>
    <param-value>true</param-value>
  </init-param>
  <init-param>
    <param-name>spnego.allow.unsecure.basic</param-name>
    <param-value>true</param-value>
  </init-param>
  <init-param>
    <param-name>spnego.login.client.module</param-name>
```

```
        <param-value>spnego-client</param-value>
    </init-param>
    <init-param>
        <param-name>spnego.krb5.conf</param-name>
        <param-value>FULL_PATH/krb5.conf</param-value>
    </init-param>
    <init-param>
        <param-name>spnego.login.conf</param-name>
        <param-value>FULL_PATH/login.conf</param-value>
    </init-param>
    <init-param>
        <param-name>spnego.preauth.username</param-name>
        <param-value>SPN_USERNAME</param-value>
    </init-param>
    <init-param>
        <param-name>spnego.preauth.password</param-name>
        <param-value>SPN_PASSWORD</param-value>
    </init-param>
    <init-param>
        <param-name>spnego.login.server.module</param-name>
        <param-value>spnego-server</param-value>
    </init-param>
    <init-param>
        <param-name>spnego.prompt.ntlm</param-name>
        <param-value>true</param-value>
    </init-param>
    <init-param>
        <param-name>spnego.logger.level</param-name>
        <param-value>1</param-value>
    </init-param>
        <init-param>
        <param-name>spnego.skip.client.internet</param-name>
        <param-value>false</param-value>
    </init-param>
</filter>
```

6. Add the following XML snippet before the `login` entry:

```
<filter-mapping>
    <filter-name>SpnegoHttpFilter</filter-name>
    <url-pattern>/*</url-pattern>
</filter-mapping>
```

7. Open the `seraph-config.xml` file located in the `<JIRA_INSTALL>`/atlassian-jira/WEB-INF/classes directory in a text editor.

8. Locate the line that contains `com.atlassian.jira.security.login.JiraSeraphAuthenticator` and comment it out so it looks like the following:

```
<!--

<authenticator class="com.atlassian.jira.security.login.
JiraSeraphAuthenticator"/>

-->
```

9. Add the following XML snippet below the line that's been commented out:

```
<authenticator class="com.appfusions.jira.SeraphAuthenticator" />
```

10. Restart JIRA.

11. Add your JIRA's URL to the **Local Intranet Zone** in your browser.

After JIRA is restarted, you should be auto-logged in every time you are logged onto the Windows domain.

Make sure you also have a backup copy of the file before making any changes.

5
JIRA Security

In this chapter, we will cover:

- ► Granting access to JIRA
- ► Granting JIRA System Administrator access
- ► Controlling access to a project
- ► Controlling access to JIRA issue operations
- ► Setting up issue-level permissions
- ► Restricting access to projects based on reporter permissions
- ► Setting up password policies
- ► Capturing electronic signatures for changes
- ► Changing the duration of the remember me cookies
- ► Changing the default session timeout

Introduction

Security is one of the most important aspects of any information system. With JIRA, this includes managing different levels of access and making sure the information can only be accessed by authorized users.

In this chapter, we will cover the different levels of access control in JIRA. We will also cover other security-related topics, including enforcing password strength and capturing and auditing changes in JIRA for regulatory compliance.

Granting access to JIRA

By default, normal users (non-administrators) need to be in the **jira-users** group to log in to JIRA. Often, as your JIRA grows, it is not feasible to have everyone in the jira-users group; for example, you might have one group for all internal employees and another group for consultants and contractors. In this case, you will need to grant permission to both the groups so that they can log in to JIRA.

In this recipe, we will be creating a new custom field from the default selection: a single select list custom field.

How to do it...

Proceed with the following steps to grant JIRA access to a group:

1. Log in to JIRA as a JIRA administrator.
2. Navigate to **Administration | User Management | Global Permissions**.
3. Select the **JIRA Users** option for the **Permission** select list and select the group you want to grant access to.
4. Click on **Add**, and this will allow users in the selected group to access JIRA.

JIRA Users Ability to log in to JIRA. They are a 'user'. Any new users created will automatically join these groups, unless those groups have JIRA System Administrators or JIRA Administrators permissions. **Note:** All users need this permission to log in to JIRA, even if they have other permissions.	• jira-users View Users · Delete jira-users groups is granted this permission by default

How it works...

The JIRA Users global permission allows users to log in to JIRA. When a user is created in JIRA, he or she will be automatically added to all groups that have this permission, unless the group also has a JIRA Administrator or JIRA System Administrators global permission. It is important to pay attention to what groups you add here so that users will not be automatically added to the groups they don't belong to.

> Users with JIRA Administrators and JIRA System Administrators global permissions can also log in to JIRA.

There's more...

Users in the groups that have the JIRA Users global permission (also JIRA Administrators and JIRA System Administrators; see the next recipe) will count towards your license limit.

Granting JIRA System Administrator access

In the previous recipe, we looked at how to grant access to JIRA to a normal user. In this recipe, we will look at how to grant users with administrator access. Just like granting user access, you can only grant administrator access to a group of users.

How to do it...

Proceed with the following steps to grant a group administrator access in JIRA:

1. Navigate to **Administration | User Management | Global Permissions**.
2. Select the **JIRA System Administrators** option for the **Permission** select list and select the group you want to grant access to, as shown in the following screenshot:

JIRA System Administrators
Ability to perform all administration functions. There must be at least one group with this permission.

Note: People with this permission can always log in to JIRA.

- jira-administrators
  View Users · Delete

jira-administrators group is granted both permissions by default

JIRA Administrators
Ability to perform most administration functions (excluding Import & Export, SMTP Configuration, etc.).

Note: People with this permission can always log in to JIRA.

- jira-administrators
  View Users · Delete

How it works...

There are two levels of administrator access in JIRA: JIRA Administrator and JIRA System Administrator. For the most part, they have identical functions when it comes to JIRA configurations such as custom fields and workflows. JIRA System Administrators have additional access to system-wide application configurations such as the SMTP mail server configuration, installing add-ons, and updating JIRA licenses.

Out of the box, the jira-administrators group has both JIRA Administrator and JIRA System Administrator global permissions. If you want to distinguish between the two different levels of administration, you can create two separate groups and grant them with different permissions.

Controlling access to a project

In the previous recipes, we looked at how to use global permissions to control JIRA access and administrator-level access. In this recipe, we will look at how to control project-level permissions, starting with access to projects.

Getting ready

To control project-level access, we use permission schemes. JIRA comes with a Default Permission Scheme, which is applied automatically to all projects. You can use this scheme and update its permission settings directly. For this recipe, we will start with creating a new permission scheme to illustrate how to create a new scheme from scratch. If you want to just use the default scheme, you can skip the first three steps.

How to do it...

We first need to create a new permission scheme, which can be done with the following steps:

1. Navigate to **Administration | Issues | Permission Schemes**.
2. Click on the **Add Permission Scheme** button.
3. Enter the new scheme's name and click on **Add**.

   With the permission scheme created, we then need to grant permissions to users, namely the **Browse Projects** permission that controls access to projects.

4. Click on the **Permissions** link for the new permission scheme.
5. Click on the **Add** link for the **Browse Projects** permission.
6. Select the permission type to apply; for example, if you want to limit access to only members of a group, you can select the **Group** option to select the target group and click on **Add**:

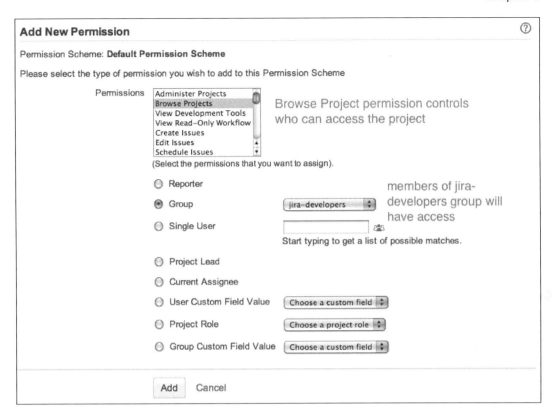

We can grant permissions to multiple users and groups, and once finished, we can apply the permission scheme to the project we want:

1. Go to the project you want to apply the permission scheme to and click on the **Administration** tab.

2. Select the **Permissions** option on the left-hand side, and click the **Use a different scheme** option from the **Actions** menu.

3. Select the new permission scheme and click on **Associate**.

How it works...

Permission schemes define project-level permissions. Unlike global permissions, which can only be granted to groups, these can be granted to specific users, groups, project roles, and more. Once configured, you can apply the scheme to individual projects. This way, different projects can have different permission schemes to suit their needs.

Controlling access to JIRA issue operations

In this recipe, we will look at permissions that control issue operations.

Getting ready

Just as we saw in the previous recipe, you can either use an existing permission scheme or create a new permission scheme. For this recipe, we will continue working with the permission scheme we have created previously.

How to do it...

Proceed with the following steps to set up permission schemes for issue operations:

1. Go to the project you want to apply the project scheme to and click on the **Administration** tab.

2. Select the **Permissions** option on the left-hand side, and click on the **Edit Permissions** option from the **Actions** menu.

3. Click on the **Add** link for permissions you want to update such as **Create Issue** and **Edit Issue**. Issue-related permissions are grouped under the **Issue Permissions** heading.

4. Select the permission type to apply and click on **Add**.

 You can select multiple permissions at once by holding down your *Shift* or *Ctrl* key while selecting.

There's more...

If in doubt or if you have users reporting permission-related issues, you can always use the **Permission Helper** tool (shown in the following screenshot) to check your configurations. All you have to do is enter the user's username, select an issue that is in the project, choose the type of permission, and click on **Submit**. The tool will go through your permission configurations and display a report that explains what is required for the selected permission, so you can work out why the user has or does not have the selected permission.

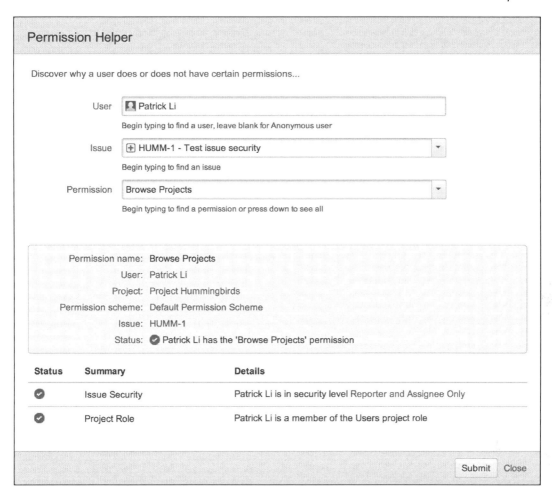

Setting up issue-level permissions

When you have a mixed group of users such as internal employees and outside consultants working on the same JIRA project, there will be issues with sensitive information that should only be viewed by internal employees. In these cases, you would want to mark those issues as internal only so other people cannot see them.

In this recipe, we will look at how to set up permissions to control access at issue level with issue security schemes.

How to do it...

The steps for setting up issue-level permissions are as follows:

1. Since JIRA does not come with any default issue security schemes, the first step is to create a new one from scratch:

    1. Navigate to **Administration | Issues | Issue Security Schemes**.
    2. Click on the **Add Issue Security Scheme** button.
    3. Enter the new scheme's name and click on **Add**.

2. The second step is to set up the security levels you can choose from, such as **Internal Users Only**:

    1. Click on the **Security Levels** link for our new issue security scheme.
    2. Enter the name for each security level and click on the **Add Security Levels** button.

    The following screenshot shows three existing security levels. You add a new security level from the form at the bottom:

Security Level	Users / Groups / Project Roles	Operations
Internal Users Only	• Group (jira-users) (Delete)	Add
		· Default
		· Delete
Internal and External Users	• Group (jira-users) (Delete)	Add
	• Group (consultants) (Delete)	· Default
	• Group (contractors) (Delete)	· Delete
Reporter and Assignee Only	• Reporter (Delete)	Add
	• Current Assignee (Delete)	· Default
		· Delete

existing security levels

Add Security Level ⑦

Add a new security level by entering a name and description below.

create a new security level

Name [   ]

Description [   ]

[Add Security Level]

You can also click on the **Default** link to make a security level default. This will preselect the default security level while creating new issues in projects using the issue security scheme.

3. After we have set up the security levels, the third step is to grant users access to each of the security levels you have defined:

   1. Click on the **Add** link for the security level you want to set up the user access for.

   2. Select the permission option and click on the **Add** button.

The following screenshot displays the different options you have while granting security levels:

Add User/Group/Project Role to Issue Security Level

Issue Security Scheme: **Default Issue Security Scheme**
Issue Security Level: **Internal Users Only**

Please select a user or group to add to this security level.
This will enable the specific users/groups to view issues for projects that:

- are associated with this Issue Security Scheme and
- have their security level set to **Internal Users Only**

○ Reporter

◉ Group   [jira-users ▴▾]

○ Single User   [   ] 🔒

○ Project Lead

○ Current Assignee

○ User Custom Field Value   [Choose a custom field ▴▾]

○ Project Role   [Choose a project role ▴▾]

○ Group Custom Field Value   [Choose a custom field ▴▾]

○ Reporter (show only projects with create permission)

[Add]   Cancel

---

4. Now that we have all the security levels set up, the last step is to apply the issue security scheme to our project:

   1. Go to the project you want to apply the issue security scheme to and click on the **Administration** tab.

   2. Select the **Issue Security** option on the left-hand side, and click on the **Select a scheme** option from the **Actions** menu.

   3. Select the new issue security scheme and click on **Next**.

   4. If the project is not empty, JIRA will ask you to select a default security level for all the issues. You can select the **None** option so that all issues will remain as is, or you can select a security level that will be applied to all issues.

   5. Click on the **Associate** button and the issue security scheme will now be applied to the project:

Associate Issue Security Scheme to Project

Step 2 of 2: Associate any issues in this project that previously had their security level set, with a security level from the new scheme.

Selecting a new level will change the security level of all the affected issues to be the newly selected security level

Security Levels for   **Security Levels for Test**   select default security level
                                                                              to apply
None (1 affected Issues)   None

                              Associate   Cancel

How it works...

The issue security scheme allows you to control who can access individual issues based on the security levels set. Issues with a security level can only be viewed by those who meet the criteria. Note that subtasks will inherit security levels from their parent issues.

Once we have applied the issue security scheme to a project, users with the **Set Issue Security** permission will be able to select a security level while creating and editing issues, as shown in the following screenshot.

If you do not see the **Security Levels** field, make sure the field is added to the screen and you have the Set Issue Security permission.

It is also worth mentioning that you can only select security levels that you belong to. For example, if there are two security levels, A and B, security level A is granted to the jira-administrators group and security level B is granted to the jira-users group. Now, as a member of the jira-users group, you will only be able to select security level B.

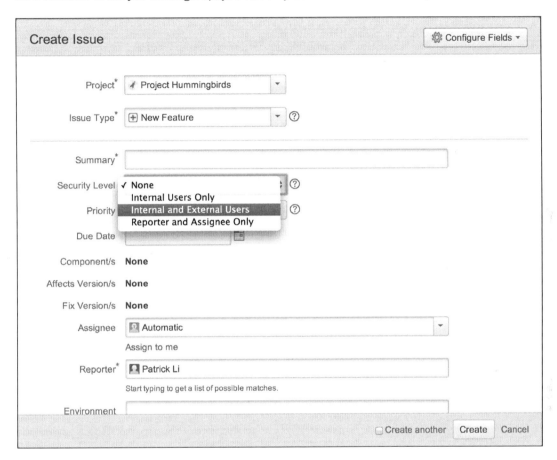

For a user who meets the criteria for the selected security level, he or she will be able to view the issue normally. However, if a user who does not meet the criteria tries to view the issue, he or she will get a permission violation error, as shown in the following screenshot:

Permission Violation

⚠ It seems that you have tried to perform an operation which you are not permitted to perform.

If you think this message is wrong, please contact your JIRA administrators.

Restricting access to projects based on reporter permissions

As we have seen in one of the previous recipes, the **Browse Projects** permission controls who can access a project in JIRA. In this recipe, we will set up permissions so that users can only see projects they can create issues in and not the projects they cannot.

Getting ready

Since we will be making direct changes to a JIRA system file, make sure you create backups for any modified files. This recipe will also require a restart of JIRA, so plan this during a time slot that will not affect your users.

How to do it...

To restrict access to projects based on who can or cannot report criterion, you will first need to enable a special permission type:

1. Open the `permission-types.xml` file from the `<JIRA_INSTALL>/atlassian-jira/WEB-INF/classes` directory in a text editor.

2. Locate the following lines and uncomment the `reportercreate` permission type:

    ```
    <!-- Uncomment & use this permission to show only projects where
    the user has create permission and issues within that where they
    are the reporter. -->
    <!-- This permission type should only ever be assigned to the
    "Browse Projects" permission. -->
    <!-- Other permissions can use the "reporter" or "create"
    permission type as appropriate. -->
    <!--
    <type id="reportercreate" enterprise="true">
    <class>com.atlassian.jira.security.type.
    CurrentReporterHasCreatePermission</class>
    </type>
    -->
    ```

3. Restart JIRA for the changes to apply.

Once the `reportercreate` permission type is enabled, there will be a new **Reporter** tab (which shows only projects with create permissions) while working with permission schemes, as shown in the following screenshot. Projects with permission schemes that use this option for the **Browse Projects** permission can only be viewed by users who can create issues in them.

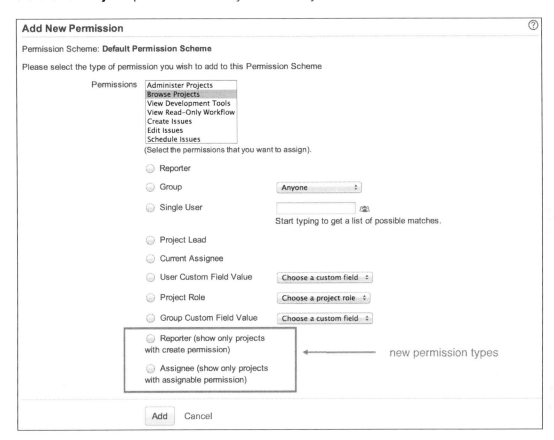

How it works...

The `reportercreate` permission type will check whether the current user has permission to create issues in a given project. This is different than the default reporter or the current reporter permission type, which will make the project visible to all users.

Also, take note that this permission should only be applied to the **Browse Projects** permission. If applied to other permissions, especially the **Create Issues** permission, it will cause JIRA to go into an infinite loop, and this is the reason why this permission type is disabled by default.

There's more...

There is also a similar **Assignee (show only projects with assignable permission)** permission type, which can be enabled in the `permission-types.xml` file. Similar to the reporter equivalent, this permission type will check whether users can be assigned issues in the project. Just like the reporter permission type, this should only be applied to the **Browse Projects** permission:

```
<!-- Uncomment & use this permission to show only projects where the
user has the assignable permission and issues within that where they
are the assignee -->
<!-- This permission type should only ever be assigned to the "Browse
Projects" permission. -->
<!-- Other permissions can use the "reporter" or "create" permission
type as appropriate. -->
<!--
<type id="assigneeassignable" enterprise="true">        <class>com.
atlassian.jira.security.type.CurrentAssigneeHasAssignablePermission</
class>
</type>
-->
```

Setting up password policies

By default, JIRA allows you to create a password of any combination and length. For security, organizations often need to have password policies such as password length and complexity to strengthen the passwords and make them difficult to guess.

In this recipe, we will look at how to set up password policies in JIRA to define the strength of passwords.

How to do it...

Proceed with the following steps to enable and configure the password policy settings:

1. Navigate to **Administration | User Management | Password Policy**.
2. Select from one of the predefined policy settings, or select the **Custom** option and configure the settings yourself.

3. Click on the **Update** button to enable the password policy, as shown in the following screenshot:

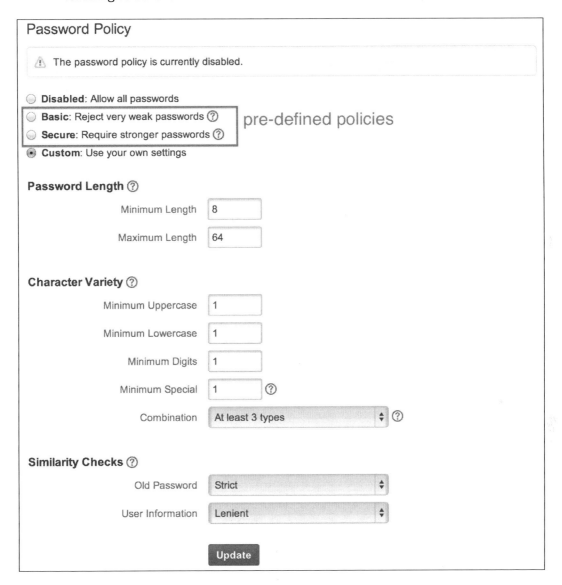

How it works...

With the password policy configured, every time someone tries to create a new password, JIRA will make sure the new password satisfies the policy rules. If it does not, error messages will be displayed with information on the requirements, as shown in the following screenshot:

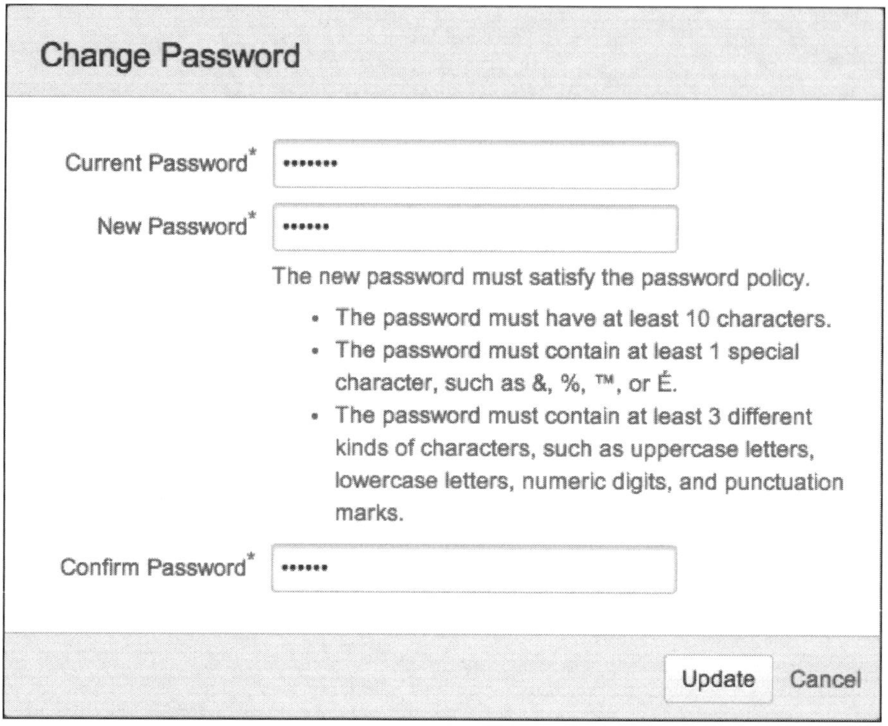

Change Password

Current Password[*] [•••••••]

New Password[*] [••••••]

The new password must satisfy the password policy.

- The password must have at least 10 characters.
- The password must contain at least 1 special character, such as &, %, ™, or É.
- The password must contain at least 3 different kinds of characters, such as uppercase letters, lowercase letters, numeric digits, and punctuation marks.

Confirm Password[*] [••••••]

[Update] Cancel

There's more...

Apart from the built-in password policy feature, there is also a third-party add-on called password policy, which provides features such as password age and user account locking. You can get the add-on from the following link:

```
https://marketplace.atlassian.com/plugins/com.intenso.jira.plugins.
password-policy
```

After you have installed the add-on in JIRA, there will be a new **Password Policy** section in **Add-ons** under **Administration**. Click on the **Configure** link and you will be able to set your password policy, as shown in the following screenshot:

> You need to disable the default password policy feature to use this add-on.

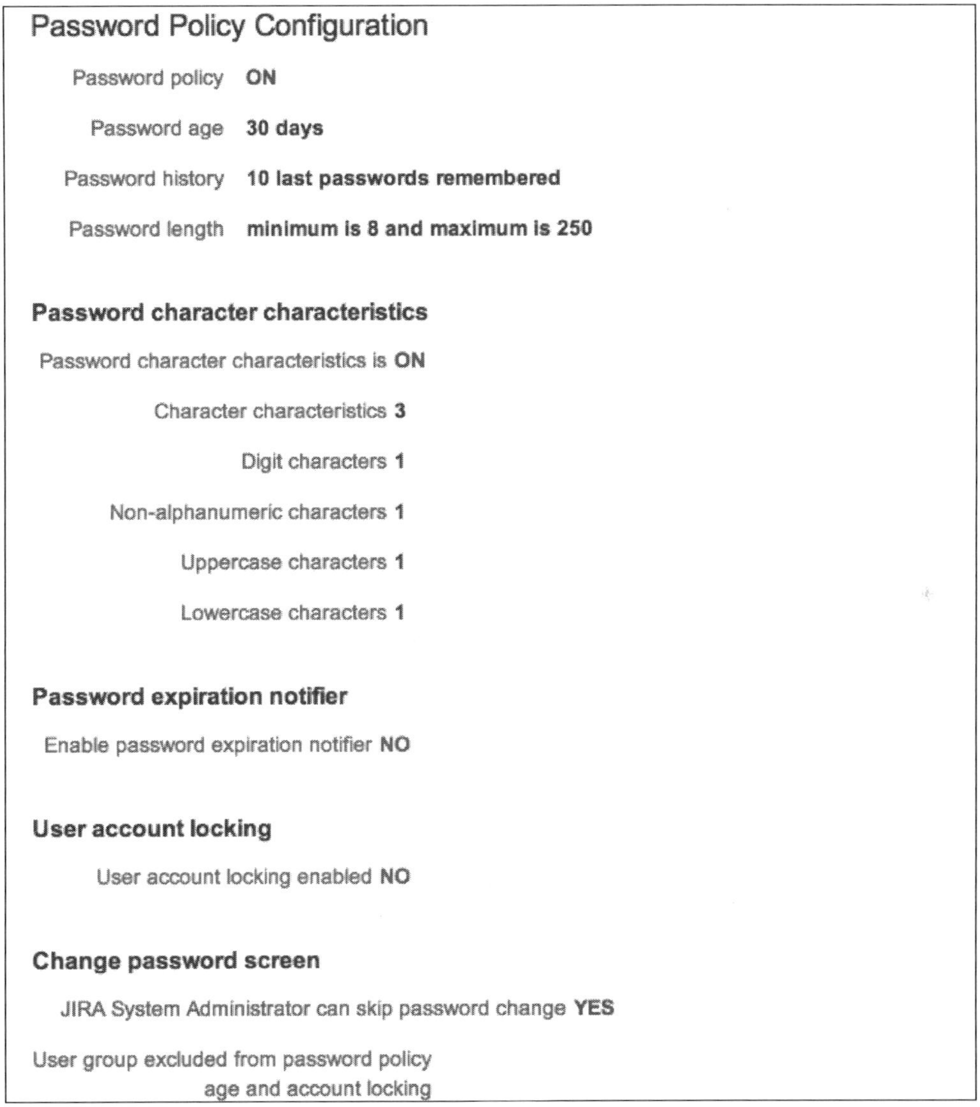

Password Policy Configuration

Password policy   **ON**

Password age   **30 days**

Password history   **10 last passwords remembered**

Password length   **minimum is 8 and maximum is 250**

Password character characteristics

Password character characteristics is **ON**

Character characteristics **3**

Digit characters **1**

Non-alphanumeric characters **1**

Uppercase characters **1**

Lowercase characters **1**

Password expiration notifier

Enable password expiration notifier **NO**

User account locking

User account locking enabled **NO**

Change password screen

JIRA System Administrator can skip password change **YES**

User group excluded from password policy age and account locking

Capturing electronic signatures for changes

Organizations that have strict regulation requirements often need to capture electronic signatures as issues move along the workflow for future auditing purposes. This is often a part of the CFR Part 11 compliance.

In this recipe, we will look at how to enforce and capture e-signatures when someone tries to transition an issue through the workflow.

Getting ready

For this recipe, we need to have the CFR Part 11 E-Signatures add-on installed. You can download the add-on from the following link:

```
http://www.appfusions.com/display/PRT11J/Home
```

How to do it...

To start capturing electronic signatures, we first need to create an **Electronic Signature** custom field:

1. Navigate to **Administration | Issues | Custom Fields**.
2. Click on the **Add Custom Field** button and select the **Advanced** tab.
3. Choose the **Electronic Signature** custom field type and click on **Next**.
4. Name the custom field E-Signatures and click on **Next**, as shown in the following screenshot.

5. Select a screen to place the custom field onto. For example, if you want to capture signatures when users resolve an issue, you will need to select the screen used for the **Resolve Issue** transition.

6. Click on the **Update** button.

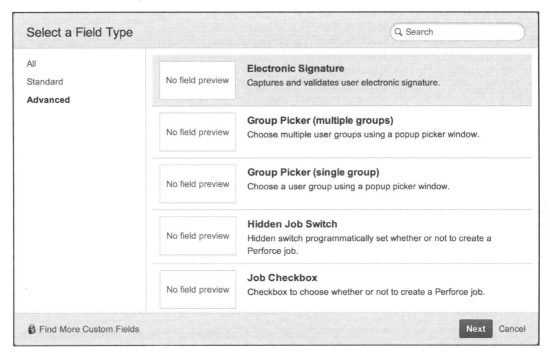

How it works...

Once you have created an **Electronic Signature** custom field and added it onto a screen, such as the **Resolve Issue** screen, it will be displayed as two text fields: one for the username and one for the password. The workflow transition can only be completed when the user signs the action by putting in his or her username and password, as shown in the following screenshot:

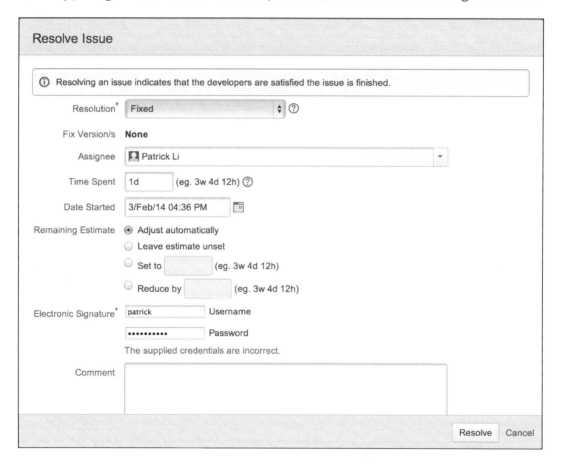

If the signature verification is successful and the transition is complete, the electronic signature will be stored, and you can get a report by clicking on the new **E-Signatures** issue tab at the bottom of the web page:

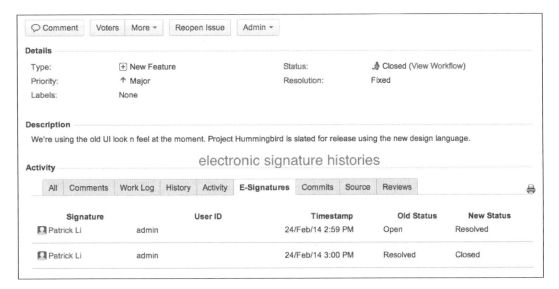

The **E-Signatures** add-on also has a **Restricted Mode** option (turned off by default), which forces users to sign the operations with their own credentials. You can enable the restricted mode by performing the following steps:

1. Navigate to **Administration | Add-ons | E-Signature Fields**.
2. Select the **Restricted Mode** option and click on **Save**.

Once enabled, the username field will be automatically set to the current user's username, so you can only sign with your own password.

Changing the duration of the remember me cookies

When a user selects the **Remember my login on this computer** option, the user will not need to re-enter their credentials again from the same browser, unless they are explicitly logged out. In addition, by default, this feature lasts for 30 days.

In this recipe, we will look at how to change the duration and extend it to the maximum extent possible.

Getting ready

Since we will be making direct changes to a JIRA system file, make sure you create backups for any files you modify. This recipe will also require a restart of JIRA, so plan this during a time slot that will not affect your users.

How to do it...

Proceed with the following steps to change the remember me cookie duration:

1. Open the `seraph-config.xml` file from the `<JIRA_INSTALL>/atlassian-jira/WEB-INF/classes` directory in a text editor.

2. Locate the following lines and change the value of `param-value` to the desired number in seconds:

```
<init-param>
    <param-name>autologin.cookie.age</param-name>
    <param-value>1209600</param-value>
</init-param>
```

3. Restart JIRA for the changes to apply.

How it works...

JIRA uses the Seraph framework (`https://docs.atlassian.com/atlassian-seraph/latest`) to manage its HTTP session cookies. When the **Remember me** option is checked, it will create a `seraph.rememberme.cookie`.

The `seraph-config.xml` file is used to configure the Seraph framework and the `autologin.cookie.age` parameter is used to set the maximum age for the cookie.

See also

Refer to the *Changing the default session timeout* recipe on how to change the default session timeout setting.

Changing the default session timeout

By default, each active user session lasts for 5 hours or 300 minutes of idle time. This means a user can log in and leave the computer for up to 5 hours and their browser session will still remain active.

In this recipe, we will look at how to change the default session timeout.

Getting ready

Since we will be making direct changes to a JIRA file, make sure you create backups for any files that are modified. This recipe will also require a restart of JIRA, so plan this during a time slot that will not affect your users.

How to do it...

Proceed with the following steps to change the session timeout settings in JIRA:

1. Open the `web.xml` file from the `<JIRA_INSTALL>/atlassian-jira/WEB-INF` directory in a text editor.

2. Locate the following lines and change the value of `session-timeout` to the desired number in minutes:

   ```
   <session-config>
       <session-timeout>300</session-timeout>
   </session-config>
   ```

3. Restart JIRA for the changes to apply.

How it works...

JIRA uses the standard Java session configuration in the `web.xml` file, which defines the session timeout in minutes. You can refer to this at the following location:

`http://docs.oracle.com/cd/E13222_01/wls/docs81/webapp/web_xml.html#1017275`

6
E-mails and Notifications

In this chapter, we will cover:

- ▶ Setting up an outgoing mail server
- ▶ Sending e-mails to users from JIRA
- ▶ Sending notifications for issue updates
- ▶ Creating custom events
- ▶ Creating custom e-mail templates
- ▶ Disabling outgoing notifications
- ▶ Creating mail handlers to process incoming e-mails
- ▶ Setting up a project-specific From address

Introduction

E-mail is one of the most important communication tools in the world. It is a technology that people are familiar with and has the least amount of resistance in regards to adoption. Therefore, e-mail integration has become one of the key features for any system today. Help desk systems, CRMs, and even document management systems all need to be able to both send and receive e-mails. So, it is not surprising that JIRA comes with a full list of e-mail integration features out of the box.

In this chapter, we will learn about how to configure JIRA to send out e-mail notifications every time someone makes a change to issues, set up notification rules, and create custom mail templates. We will also look at how JIRA can process e-mails and create issues automatically, saving us the effort of manual data entry.

Setting up an outgoing mail server

In this recipe, we will look at how to set up an outgoing mail server in JIRA that can be used to send direct e-mails to users or automated notifications for changes to issues.

How to do it...

Proceed with the following steps to set up an outgoing mail server:

1. Log in to JIRA as a JIRA administrator.
2. Navigate to **Administration | System | Outgoing Mail**.
3. Click on the **Configure new SMTP mail server** button.
4. Set a name for the mail server; for example, you can use the mail server's hostname.
5. Select the **From address** field that will be used when users receive an e-mail from JIRA.
6. Provide an **Email prefix** value, which will be added to every e-mail's subject; for example, you can use JIRA to let users know it is coming from JIRA.
7. Select whether you will be using a custom SMTP server or either Gmail or Yahoo! mail. If you are using Gmail or Yahoo!, make sure you select the corresponding option and provide the access credentials. If you are using a custom SMTP server, you will need to provide its hostname, port number, and credentials, if necessary.
8. Click on the **Test Connection** button, with the credentials provided, to make sure JIRA is able to connect to the mail server. If the test is successful, click on the **Add** button, as shown in the following screenshot:

Add SMTP Mail Server

Use this page to add a new SMTP mail server. This server will be used to send all outgoing mail from JIRA.

Name * `Gmail`
The name of this server within JIRA.

Description `                    `

From address * `no-reply@appfusions.`
The default address this server will use to send emails from.

Email prefix * `[JIRA]`
This prefix will be prepended to all outgoing email subjects.

Server Details
Enter *either* the host name of your SMTP server *or* the JNDI location of a javax.mail.Session object to use.

SMTP Host

Service Provider

| Custom |
| ✓ Google Apps Mail / Gmail |
| Yahoo! Mail Plus |

Timeout `10000`
Timeout in milliseconds - 0 or negative values indicate infinite timeout. Leave blank for default (10000 ms).

Username `          `
Optional - if you use authenticated SMTP to send email, enter your username.

Password `          `
Optional - as above, enter your password if you use authenticated SMTP.

or

JNDI Location

JNDI Location `          `
The JNDI location of a javax.mail.Session object, which has already been set up in JIRA's application server.

Test Connection Add Cancel

 You can have only one outgoing mail server.

Once we have configured the outgoing mail server in JIRA, we can send a test e-mail to make sure everything is working properly:

1. Click on the **Send a Test Email** link.

2. Verify whether the e-mail address in the **To** field is one that you have access to.

3. Click on the **Send** button to send the test e-mail.

JIRA will immediately send out the test e-mail (normal notification e-mails are placed in a queue before sending) to the address in the **To** field, with the subject and body content specified. If there is an error, you can check the SMTP logging checkbox to get more details on the error:

Send Email

You can send a test email here.

To	patrick@appfusions.com
Subject	Test Message From JIRA
Message Type	Text ◆
Body	This is a test message from JIRA. Server: Gmail SMTP Port: 465 Description: From: no–reply@appfusions.com Host User Name: dragonite40@gmail.com
SMTP logging	☐ Log SMTP-level details

Send   Cancel

Mail log

Log	Your test message has been sent successfully to patrick@appfusions.com. email successfully sent

Log of the events for sending mail.

Sending e-mails to users from JIRA

With the outgoing mail server set up, we are now able to send e-mails directly from JIRA. One common use case is to send out reminders such as system maintenance notices to everyone in JIRA, or sending important updates to members of a project. In this recipe, we will look at how to perform these types of tasks with JIRA.

Getting ready

You must first configure an outgoing mail server for JIRA. Refer to the previous recipe, *Setting up an outgoing mail server*, for details.

How to do it...

Proceed with the following steps to send out direct e-mails to users in JIRA:

1. Navigate to **Administration | System | Send Email**.
2. Select the recipients of the e-mail. You can choose to send an e-mail via **Project Roles** or **Groups**. For example, to send an e-mail to everyone who uses JIRA, you can select the **jira-users** group (if it is the group that people need to be in, in order to use JIRA).
3. Type in your e-mail subject and body.
4. Check the **Bcc** checkbox if you do not want people to see other recipients' e-mail addresses.
5. Click on the **Send** button to send the e-mail, as shown in the following screenshot:

Send Email

You can send an email to JIRA users here.

Please select one or more groups or project roles from the list below. The email message will be sent to all members of the chosen groups or project roles.
Note: a user will receive the email only once, even if they are a member of more than one group or project role.

From	dragonite40@hotmail.com
To *	○ Project Roles ● Groups
	Groups: jira-administrators jira-developers jira-users
Reply To	
	Optionally, specify the 'Reply-To' address.
Subject *	JIRA maintenance this weekend
Body *	Hi all, JIRA will be unavailable between this Saturday 9AM – Sunday 5PM, as part of planned upgrade. IT Team
	The body of the email message. You may include HTML.
Message Type	HTML ⬍
	The content-type of the email message.
Bcc	☑
	Check this box if you want to hide the users email address.

Send   Cancel

Sending notifications for issue updates

The other major use of outgoing mails is for JIRA to automatically send out notifications about changes to issues; for example, if an issue has been updated, you would want the issue's reporter and assignee to be notified of the change.

In this recipe, we will look at how to set up notification rules so that interested parties are notified of any changes to their issues.

Getting ready

You must first configure an outgoing mail server for JIRA. Refer to the *Setting up an outgoing mail server* recipe for details.

How to do it...

JIRA uses notification schemes to control who should receive notifications for a given event. JIRA comes with a **Default Notification Scheme**; you can choose to update this scheme directly by clicking on the **Notifications** link. In this recipe, however, we will be creating a new notification scheme and applying that to projects:

1. Proceed with the following steps to create a new notification scheme:
    1. Navigate to **Administration | Issues | Notification Scheme**.
    2. Click on the **Add Notification Scheme** button.
    3. Enter a name for the new scheme and click on **Add** to create it.

   After you have created a new notification scheme, you will be taken to the **Notifications** settings page for the scheme. By default, there will be no notifications set for any events, as shown in the following screenshot:

Event	Notifications	Operations
Issue Created (System)	• Reporter (Delete)	Add
events	• Current Assignee (Delete) notification recipients	
	• All Watchers (Delete)	
Issue Updated (System)	• Single Email Address (patrick@appfusions.com) (Delete)	Add
	• User Custom Field Value (CC) (Delete)	
Issue Assigned (System)		Add
Issue Resolved (System)		Add

2. To add a notification recipient to an event, proceed with the following steps:
    1. Click on the **Add** link for the event.
    2. Select the notification recipient type and click on **Add**.

You can add a notification recipient to multiple events at the same time by using the multiselect events field.

You can add as many notification recipients as you need for an event, and JIRA will make sure not to send duplicated e-mails to the same user. For example, if you have set both the reporter and assignee to receive notifications for a single event, and they happen to be the same user, JIRA will only send out one e-mail instead of two.

Also note that JIRA will take permissions into consideration while sending out notifications. If a user does not have access to the issue, JIRA will not send notifications to that user. The following screenshot of the **Add Notification** page denotes this:

Add Notification ⑦

Notification Scheme: **Default Notification Scheme**

Please select the type of Notification you wish to add to scheme:

Events
> Issue Created
> Issue Updated
> Issue Assigned   ← you can select more than
> Issue Resolved   one events
> Issue Closed
> Issue Commented
> Issue Comment Edited

(Select the notifications that you want to assign)

○ Current Assignee

○ Reporter

○ Current User

○ Project Lead

○ Component Lead

who should be   ○ Single User   [   ] 👥
notified for the   Start typing to get a list of possible matches.
selected event(s)
                       ○ Group   [Choose a group   ⬍]

                       ○ Project Role   [Choose a project role ⬍]

                       ○ Single Email Address [   ]
                                              Notifications will be sent **only** for public issues. Public issues
                                              are issues which have a Permission scheme that gives the
                                              'Browse Projects' permission to 'Anyone'(any non-logged-in
                                              users).

                       ○ All Watchers

                       ○ User Custom Field   [Choose a custom field ⬍]
                       Value

                       ○ Group Custom Field   [Choose a custom field ⬍]
                       Value

[Add]   Cancel

3. The last step is to apply our new notification scheme to a project:

    1. Browse to the project you want to apply the notification scheme to.

    2. Click on the **Administration** tab.

    3. Select the **Notifications** option from the left panel.

    4. Select **Use a different scheme** from the **Actions** menu.

    5. Select **New Notification Scheme** and click on **Associate**.

How it works...

JIRA uses an event system where every issue operation such as creating a new issue or workflow transitions will all trigger a corresponding event to be fired. As we have seen, notification schemes map events to notification recipients. This way, we are able to set up flexible notification rules to notify different people for different events.

JIRA provides many different notification recipient types. Some are very simple, such as **Current Assignee and Reporter**, which will simply take the current value of those fields. Other options such as **User Custom Field Value** can be very powerful. For example, you can create a multiuser picker custom field, and for each issue, you can have a different list of users as recipients, without having to modify the actual scheme itself.

Events are also mapped to e-mail templates so JIRA knows what to use for the subject and body. You cannot change the mapping for system events, but as we will see in the next recipe, we can create custom events and select what templates to use.

Creating custom events

In the previous recipe, *Sending notifications for issue updates*, we looked at how to set up notification schemes by mapping events to notification recipients.

In this recipe, we will expand on that and look at how to create our custom events. This has two obvious advantages:

▶ We can map our own e-mail templates to these custom events

▶ We can specify exactly what event will be fired for each workflow transition and set up notification rules accordingly

How to do it...

Proceed with the following steps to create custom events in JIRA:

1. Navigate to **Administration | System | Events**.

2. Enter the new event's name.

3. Select a template that will be used for the e-mail notification when the event is fired. You can select from a list of JIRA-bundled templates or the custom templates you created.

4. Click on the **Add** button to create the new event, as shown in the following screenshot:

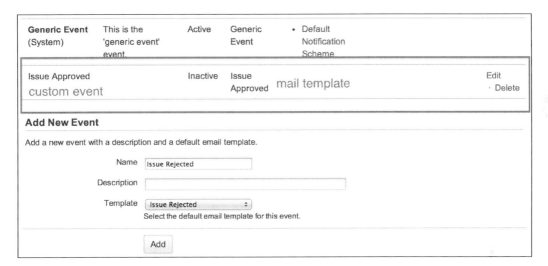

Once you have created the events, they will be available in notification schemes, and we will be able to select who will receive e-mail notifications, as shown in the following screenshot:

Issue Worklog Deleted (System)	• Current Assignee (Delete) • Reporter (Delete) • All Watchers (Delete)	Add
Generic Event (System) custom events in notification scheme	• Current Assignee (Delete) • Reporter (Delete) • All Watchers (Delete)	Add
Issue Approved	• Reporter (Delete)	Add
Issue Rejected	• Reporter (Delete)	Add

The last step is to make sure our custom events are fired when users trigger the action:

1. Navigate to **Administration | Issues | Workflows**.

2. Click on the **Edit** link for the workflow, which contains the transitions that will fire the custom event. In this case, we will be using a simple **Approval Workflow** that contains a transition called **Approve**:

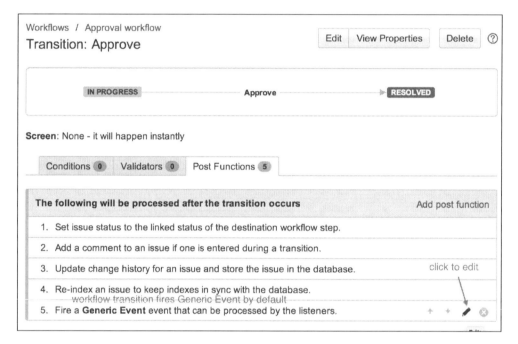

3. Click on the workflow transition and select the **Post Functions** tab. Normally, you will see the last post function in the list firing **Generic Event**.

4. Hover your mouse over the post function and click on the edit icon (it looks like a pencil).

5. Select the new custom event and click on **Update** as shown in the following screenshot. This will make the transition to fire our event instead of the default **Generic Event**.

Update parameters of the Fire Event Function for this transition.

Update parameters of the Fire Event Function for this transition.

Event: Issue Approved

The event to fire.

Update   Cancel

How it works...

Unlike system events, custom events can only be fired from workflow transitions, so we have to update our workflows. Every workflow transition fires an event, and by default, **Generic Event** is fired. This means most workflow transitions will have the same notification recipient using the e-mail template.

By configuring the workflow to fire our own custom event, we have finer control over who will receive notifications and what templates to use, as we will see in the next recipe, *Creating custom e-mail templates*.

Creating custom e-mail templates

So far, we have seen how to set up notification rules and create custom events. The last part of the puzzle is the e-mail templates used by JIRA while sending out notifications.

In this recipe, we will create our own e-mail templates that can be used by custom events.

How to do it...

All mail templates are stored in the **<JIRA_INSTALL>/atlassian-jira/WEB-INF/classes/templates/email** directory, and generally, for each event in JIRA, there are three template files:

- ▶ **The Subject template**: This is the template file for the e-mail's subject line, which is stored in the `subject` subdirectory
- ▶ **The Text template**: This is the template file for e-mails sent in the text format, which is stored in the `text` subdirectory
- ▶ **The HTML template**: This is the template file for e-mails sent in the HTML format, which is stored in the `html` subdirectory

To start creating our own e-mail templates, we first need to create the three files mentioned in the previous list of template files and place them in their respective directories. Take special note that all three files need to have the same filename with a `.vm` extension.

We will start with the subject template as follows:

1. Create a new file with the following code snippet:.

```
#disable_html_escaping()
$eventTypeName - ($issue.key) $issue.summary
```

2. We now need to create the body of the e-mail, keeping in mind that we have to create two versions: one for text and one for HTML. The following snippet shows the HTML version; for the text version, simply remove the HTML markups:

```
#disable_html_escaping()
Hello $issue.reporterUser.displayName,
<p>
Your request <a href="">$issue.key</a> has been approved, with the
comment below:
</p>
<blockquote>
<p>
$comment.body
</p>
</blockquote>
<br/>
Internal IT team
```

3. After we have created all three template files, we need to register them in JIRA so that they can be selected while creating custom events. To register new e-mail templates, open the `email-template-id-mappings.xml` file in a text editor; you can find the file inside the `<JIRA_INSTALL>/atlassian-jira/WEB-INF/classes` directory.

4. The `email-template-id-mappings.xml` file lists all e-mail templates in JIRA, so we need to add a new entry at the end as follows:

```
<templatemapping id="10002">
    <name>Issue Rejected</name>
    <template>issuerejected.vm</template>
    <templatetype>issueevent</templatetype>
</templatemapping>
```

There are a few points to note here:

▸ The template ID value needs to be unique.

▸ You can give any value to the `<name>` element, but it is good practice to keep it consistent with your event in JIRA.

▸ The `<template>` element should have the name of the custom template files we have created. Since we can have only one `<template>` element, all three files need to have the same filename.

▸ The `<templatetype>` element needs to have the value of `issueevent`.

Once you have added the entry and saved the file, you will need to restart JIRA for the changes to be applied.

How it works...

JIRA's e-mail templates use the Apache Velocity (`http://velocity.apache.org`) template language to display dynamic data. Each template is a mix of static text (with or without HTML markups) and some Velocity code. If you do not need to have dynamic contents, then you can have only static text in your templates.

In our previous examples, every time you see the dollar sign ($), such as `$issue.key`, it is a piece of Velocity code. The `$` sign indicates getting a variable from the Velocity context, and the variable name is the word that comes directly after the `$` sign; so, in this case, it is `issue`. The period (`.`) means getting the value specified from the variable. So, `$issue.key` can be read as "get the value of key from the variable issue", or in other words, "get me the issue's key".

JIRA exposes a number of variables in its Velocity context for e-mail templates; you can find the full list at `https://confluence.atlassian.com/display/JIRA041/Velocity+Context+for+Email+Templates`.

So, if we take a look at our templates, for the subject template, the `($issue.key) $issue.summary` Velocity code will be turned into something like `(TP-12) Request for JIRA administrator access`, where `TP-12` replaces `$issue.key` and `Request for JIRA administrator access` replaces `$issue.summary`.

The following screenshot shows a sample e-mail from the custom template we have created:

There's more...

There is an add-on called Outgoing Email Template Editor for JIRA which lets you edit existing templates directly within JIRA's web interface, without having to download and upload the files to the server. You will still have to restart JIRA however. You can get the add-on from the following link:

```
https://marketplace.atlassian.com/plugins/com.atlassian.labs.jira.
emaileditor.emaileditor-jira-plugin
```

Once you have installed the add-on, proceed with the following steps to edit templates in JIRA:

1. Navigate to **Administration** | **System** | **Email Editor**.

2. Select the template you want to edit from the left panel, and you will see its content displayed in a syntax-highlighted editor.

3. Update the template and click on the **Save** button, as shown in the following screenshot.

4. Restart JIRA to apply the change.

HTML TEMPLATES	
contactadministrator.vm	
emailfromadmin.vm	
filtersubscription.vm	
forgotpassword.vm	
forgotusernames.vm	
issueassigned.vm	
issueclosed.vm	
issuecommented.vm	
issuecommentedited.vm	
issuecreated.vm	
issuedeleted.vm	
issuegenericevent.vm	
issuementioned.vm	
issuemoved.vm	
issuenotify.vm	
issuereopened.vm	

Editing issueassigned.vm

```
1  #* @vtlvariable name="changelog" type="org.ofbiz.core.entity.GenericValue" *#
2  #* @vtlvariable name="changelogauthor"
   type="com.atlassian.jira.user.ApplicationUser" *#
3  #* @vtlvariable name="changelogauthorkey" type="java.lang.String" *#
4  #* @vtlvariable name="remoteUser" type="com.atlassian.crowd.embedded.api.User" *#
5  #disable_html_escaping()
6
7  #defaultMailHeaderWithParam("jira.email.assigned.issue.to", $changelogauthor,
   "#authorlinkkey($issue.assigneeId $linkstyle)")
8
9  #if ($comment)
10     #parse('templates/email/html/includes/patterns/comment-top.vm')
11 #end
12
13 #rowWrapperNormal("#parse('templates/email/html/includes/patterns/issue-
   title.vm')")
14
15 #if ($changelog)
16     #set
   ($changelogBody="#parse('templates/email/html/includes/fields/changelog.vm')")
17     #rowWrapperNormal($changelogBody)
18 #end
19
20 #set ($commentActionBody="#parse('templates/email/html/includes/patterns/comment-
   action.vm')")
21 #rowWrapperNormal($commentActionBody)
22
23 #parse("templates/email/html/includes/footer.vm")
24
```

Save

Disabling outgoing notifications

This recipe shows you how to completely prevent JIRA from sending out e-mails. You may need to do this if you are performing testing, data migration, or cloning a new development instance and do not want to flood users with hundreds of test notifications.

How to do it...

Proceed with the following steps to disable outgoing notifications in JIRA:

1. Navigate to **Administration | System | Outgoing Mail**.
2. Click on the **Disable Outgoing Mail** button.

Once you have disabled outgoing mails, JIRA will no longer send out notifications.

Creating mail handlers to process incoming e-mails

JIRA is not only able to send mails to users, but also to poll and process e-mails, and it can create issues or add comments to the existing issues. When set up correctly, this can be a powerful way to let your users interact with JIRA.

In this recipe, we will set up JIRA to poll incoming mails so that it can create new issues and add comments to the existing issues. This is useful in a help desk scenario where customers can write e-mails to the company's support e-mail address and let JIRA automatically create issues from them.

Getting ready...

Since JIRA will be polling e-mails from an inbox, you need to have its connection details, including:

- What protocol does it support? (for example, POP or IMAP)
- Authentication details

How to do it...

The first step to configure JIRA to process incoming e-mails is to set up the inboxes that JIRA will use to poll e-mails from:

1. Navigate to **Administration | System | Incoming Mail**.
2. Click on the **Add POP/IMAP mail server** button.
3. Click on the **Test Connection** button, with the credentials provided, to make sure JIRA is able to connect to the mail server. If the test is successful, click on the **Add** button.

After we have set up the mail inbox, we can set up what is known as mail handlers in JIRA to poll and process e-mails. In this recipe, we will use the most common handler to create and/or comment on issues from e-mail contents:

1. Click on the **Add incoming mail handler** button.
2. Enter a name for the mail handler.
3. Select **Support Inbox** from the **Server** drop-down list.
4. Set the **Delay** timer in minutes for how often the handler should poll for new e-mails. Generally, you do not want to set the time too short.
5. Select the **Create a new issue or add a comment to an existing issue** handler.
6. Click on the **Next** button to configure the mail handler, as shown in the following screenshot:

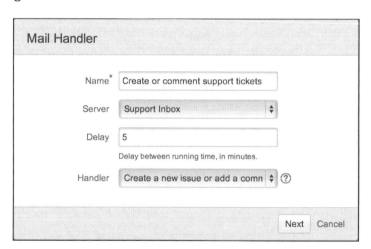

7. Enter the mail handler configuration details. The most important configurations are as follows:

    ❏ **Project**: You can only select one project. All e-mails from the inbox will go into the project selected.

    ❏ **Issue Type**: This is the issue type from which new issues will be created.

    ❏ **Create Users**: Check this if you want to automatically create a new account based on the e-mails from the addresses. Note that this would count towards your license seat.

    ❏ **Default Reporter**: If you do not want to create new accounts, you can set a use case that will be the reporter for all new issues created from e-mails.

8. Click on the **Add** button to create the mail handler.

Parameter	Description
Project	This is where the project's new issues will be created. Note that this is only used for creating new issues. While adding comments, this is ignored as comments will be added to the issue key specified in the subject.
Issue Type	This is the issue type for all newly created issues.
Strip Quotes	If this option is checked, the text wrapped in quotes will not be used as an issue description or comment.
Catch Email Address	E-mails with the specified address will be processed in this option.
Bulk	This option selects how to process autogenerated e-mails such as e-mails from JIRA. This is to prevent creating a loop where JIRA sends e-mails to the same inbox it is polling the e-mails from.
Forward Email	This option sets an address for JIRA to forward all e-mails it cannot process.
Create Users	This option creates a new user if the sender's e-mail address cannot be found.
Default Reporter	This option sets the user that will be used as the reporter if the sender's e-mail address cannot be found.
Notify Users	Uncheck this option if you do not want JIRA to send account-related e-mails.
CC Assignee	Check this option if you want the first user in the CC list to be the issue's assignee, in case a matching account can be found.
CC Watchers	Check this option if you want to add the CC list as watchers to the issue, in case matching accounts can be found.

The following screenshot shows the previously described parameters:

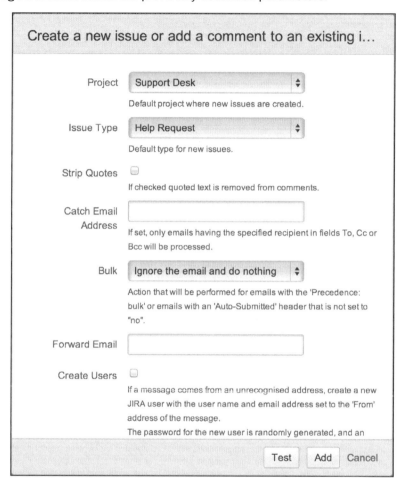

How it works...

Mail handlers periodically poll for new e-mails from the selected incoming mail server and process them based on the handler used. The **Create a new issue or add a comment to an existing issue** handler will create a new issue in JIRA, where the e-mail subject becomes the issue summary and the e-mail body becomes the issue description. If the e-mail subject contains an issue key to an existing issue, the e-mail body will be added as a comment to the issue.

JIRA comes with a number of other mail handlers:

- ▶ Add a comment from the non-quoted e-mail body—this adds the e-mail body that is not quoted with the **>** or **|** symbols as a comment to an existing issue.

- ▶ Add a comment with the entire e-mail body—this adds the entire e-mail body as a comment to an existing issue.

- ▶ Create a new issue from each e-mail message—always create a new issue from an e-mail.

- ▶ Add a comment before a specified marker or a separator in the e-mail body—this adds the e-mail body *before* a marker line is specified as a regular expression. Contents *after* the marker will be ignored. This is useful when you do not want to include old contents from a forwarded e-mail.

There is more...

JIRA's out-of-the-box mail handlers mostly focus on creating new issues from e-mails or adding comments to the existing issues based on certain matching criteria. This means that for each project, you will need to have a corresponding inbox. There are several other notable limitations, including:

- ▶ Not able to update issue fields

- ▶ Mapping one handler to multiple projects

- ▶ Notifying users that do not count towards JIRA licenses (non jira-users)

Luckily, there is a third-party add-on called Enterprise Mail Handler for JIRA, which addresses all these gaps and more. You can download the add-on from the following link:

```
https://marketplace.atlassian.com/plugins/com.javahollic.jira.jemh-ui
```

Setting up a project-specific From address

By default, all notifications sent from JIRA will have the same **From** address, configured as a part of the outgoing mail server. However, it is possible to override this on a project level, so each project can have its own From address. This can be very useful if you want to let users reply directly to notifications and have the reply added as a comment.

How to do it...

Proceed with the following steps to set up a project-specific From address:

1. Browse to the project from which you want to set up a specific From address.
2. Click on the **Administration** tab.
3. Click on the pencil (edit) icon for the **Email in Notifications** section.
4. Enter the e-mail address dedicated to the project.
5. Click on **Update** to apply the changes.

 You can revert to the default values by leaving the field blank.

The following screenshot shows the message that is displayed after we set up a project-specific From address:

 Notifications

JIRA can notify the appropriate people of particular events in your project, e.g. "Issue Commented". You can choose specific people, groups, or roles to receive notifications.

Scheme: Default Notification Scheme

Email: 🖊 hummingbirds@company.com

7
Integrating with JIRA

In this chapter, we will cover:

- ▶ Integrating Atlassian applications via application links
- ▶ Integrating JIRA with Confluence
- ▶ Integrating JIRA with other JIRA instances
- ▶ Integrating JIRA with Bamboo for build management
- ▶ Integrating JIRA with Stash
- ▶ Integrating JIRA with Bitbucket and GitHub
- ▶ Integrating JIRA with HipChat
- ▶ Creating navigation links with other applications
- ▶ Integrating JIRA with Google Drive
- ▶ Using JIRA webhooks

Introduction

The old **do it alone** approach is no longer applicable in today's IT environment. Applications and platforms need to work together in order to meet the needs of organizations. For this reason, the ability to integrate JIRA with other applications has become ever more important.

You can integrate applications with JIRA in many ways. JIRA itself comes with support to integrate with other Atlassian applications and a number of other popular **Software as a Service** (**SaaS**) applications, such as GitHub. Other than the integration supported out of the box, there are also many third-party add-ons that provide integration with applications and platforms such as Google Drive. And lastly, there is webhooks, a relatively new approach which allows any other application to register with JIRA for callbacks when certain events occur.

Integrating Atlassian applications via application links

If you need to integrate JIRA with other Atlassian applications such as Confluence or Bamboo, you should look no further than the built-in **Application Link** (or AppLink) feature. With application links, you can easily share information and access one application's feature from another application. For example, an application allows you to do the following:

- ▶ It aggregates updates into a single activity stream
- ▶ It creates JIRA issues directly from Confluence pages
- ▶ It views source code commits that are related to the current issue
- ▶ It creates branches in your code repository directly from issues

In this recipe, we will go through the steps of creating an application link between JIRA and Confluence. If you want to link JIRA with other applications such as Stash, the steps remain the same.

How to do it...

Perform the following steps to create an application link between two Atlassian applications:

1. Log in to JIRA as a JIRA administrator.
2. Navigate to **Administration | Add-ons | Application Links**.
3. Enter the URL for the target system and click on **Create new link** (this is shown in the following screenshot). JIRA will validate the URL and attempt to autodetermine the type of the target system.

Once JIRA has successfully validated the URL, if the target application type can be automatically determined, a summary for both applications will be displayed.

Make sure you use unique, fully qualified URLs; if both applications are running on the same server, that is, `example.com:8080` (for JIRA) and `example.com:8090` (for Confluence), they will not work.

From here, we need to select whether the applications have the same set of users:

1. Select the **The servers have the same set of users and usernames** checkbox. This is usually the case if both applications are using LDAP or Atlassian Crowd.

2. Select the **I am an administrator on both instances** checkbox. This will automatically redirect you to the target application and create a reciprocal link back to JIRA.

3. Click on **Continue** to create the application link in JIRA, as shown in the following screenshot:

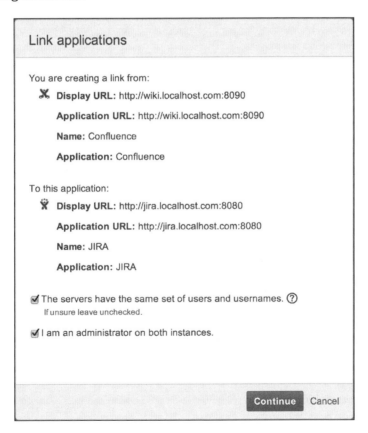

At this point, the link going out from JIRA to the target application is created. JIRA will then prompt you to create the reciprocal link; this is shown in the following screenshot:

How it works...

Application Links or AppLinks is the technology used to integrate JIRA with other Atlassian products, such as Confluence and Stash. With AppLinks, you can share information and functions between the linked applications; for example, you can link your JIRA issue with a Wiki page in Confluence or code commits in Stash.

There are a few important things to note while using AppLinks. First, you can have multiple links of the same application type, that is, you can link to multiple Confluence instances. In these cases, one of the links will be the **primary link**. The primary link will be the default application when JIRA accesses data.

Secondly, there is the authentication option. AppLinks supports three different types of authentications: Trusted Applications, OAuth, and Basic Access, all of which are shown in the following screenshot:

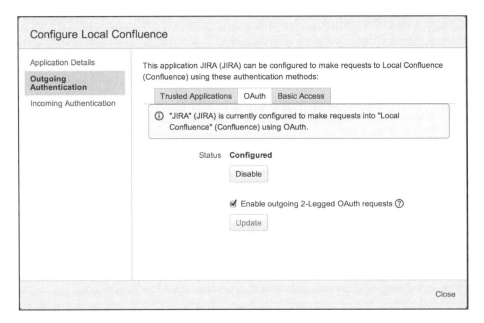

The available authentication options are as follows:

Authentication option	Description
Trusted Applications	This option is chosen if the linked applications have the same set of users, for example, if you are using LDAP or Atlassian Crowd for user management and both applications fully trust each other. With this option, users will not be required to go through an initial authorization process.
	While using trusted applications, user A from JIRA will access the target application as user A, matched via the username.
OAuth	This option is chosen if the linked applications do not have the same set of users, for example, if each application maintains its own user repository.
	With this option, users will need to go through an initial authorization process before JIRA is able to access data from the target application.
	If you are running JIRA 6.1 or newer, there is a new 2-legged OAuth option.
Basic Access	This is the simplest authentication type, where you specify a user for JIRA to use while accessing data from the target application. The access permission will be purely based on the specified user account.

Integrating JIRA with Confluence

In the previous recipe, we looked at how to use Application Links to link other Atlassian applications with JIRA. In this recipe, we will expand on this by linking JIRA with Confluence—the enterprise collaboration platform.

Getting ready

Since we will be using Confluence in this recipe, you will need to have an instance of Confluence running on your system. If you do not have one, you can download a free Confluence trial from `https://www.atlassian.com/software/confluence`.

How to do it...

The first step is to establish the link between JIRA and Confluence:

1. Navigate to **Administration | Add-ons | Application Links**.
2. Enter your Confluence URL and create the application link. JIRA should automatically detect the target application as Confluence; if, for some reason, it does not, make sure you select **Confluence** as the **Application Type** when prompted.

We also need to enable the Remote access API (disabled by default) in Confluence:

1. Log in to Confluence as a Confluence administrator.
2. Navigate to **Administration | General Configuration**.
3. Click on **Edit**, scroll down, and check the **Remote API (XML-RPC and SOAP)** option.
4. Click on **Save** to apply the change.

How it works...

After we have linked JIRA with Confluence, there will be a new option called **Confluence Page**, which appears when you select the **Link** option in the **More issues** menu:

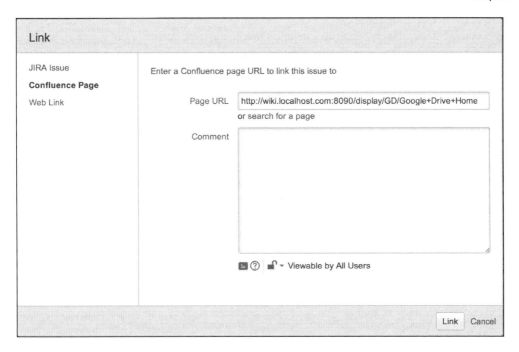

If you know the exact URL to the Confluence page, you can enter it in the **Page URL** field, or click on the **search for a page** link and search for the page you want to link to:

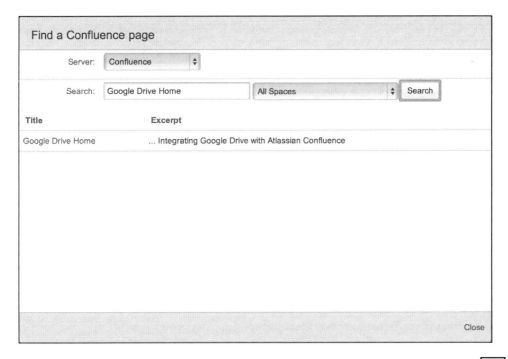

Once you have found the page you want, simply click on it and then click on the **Link** button. Linked pages will be shown under the **Issue Links** section, above the **Wiki Page** category:

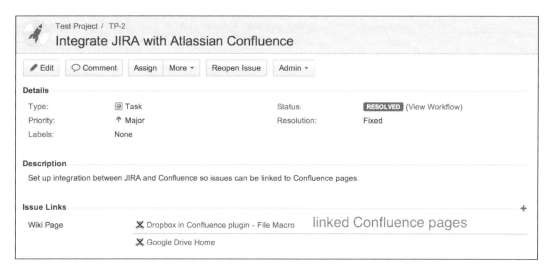

Integrating JIRA with other JIRA instances

If you have multiple JIRA instances in your organization, it is sometimes useful to integrate them together, especially when teams from different projects need to collaborate and work together. In this recipe, we will integrate two JIRA instances together so we can link issues across systems.

How to do it...

Perform the following steps to link two JIRA instances together:

1. Navigate to **Administration | Add-ons | Application Links**.

2. Enter the other JIRA's URL and create the application link. JIRA should automatically detect the target application as JIRA. If, for some reason, it does not, make sure you select **JIRA** as the **Application Type** when prompted.

How it works...

Once you have integrated two JIRA instances together with an application link, you will be able to search for and link issues from the remote JIRA instance to issues in the local JIRA instance. As shown in the following screenshot, when you use the link feature, JIRA will prompt you to select the JIRA instance that you want to search for issues to link to:

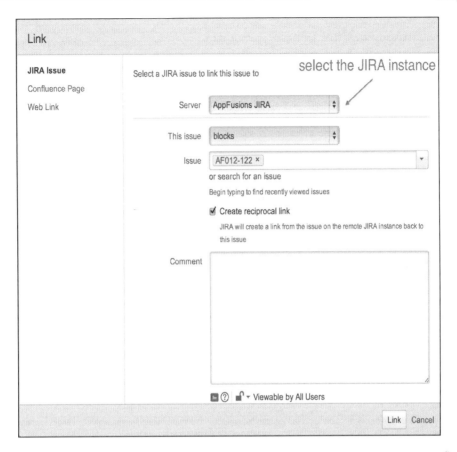

Integrating JIRA with Bamboo for build management

Bamboo is the continuous integration and build server from Atlassian. If your development team is using Bamboo, you can integrate it with JIRA and have your build plans as part of your release process.

Getting ready

Since we will be using Bamboo in this recipe, you will need to have a Bamboo instance running. If you do not have one, you can download a free Bamboo trial from `https://www.atlassian.com/software/bamboo`.

How to do it...

Since we are connecting to another Atlassian application here, we should take advantage of application links:

1. Navigate to **Administration | Add-ons | Application Links**.
2. Enter your Bamboo URL and create the application link. JIRA should automatically detect the target application as Bamboo. If, for some reason, it does not, make sure you select **Bamboo** as the **Application Type** when prompted.

How it works...

Once you have integrated JIRA and Bamboo, you will be able to run and release build plans directly from JIRA. All you have to do is select the version to release and select the **Build and Release** option.

From the release dialog shown in the following screenshot, you can select which build plan to use and run the build by clicking on the **Release** button. If the build is successful, JIRA will automatically mark the version as released once the build is completed.

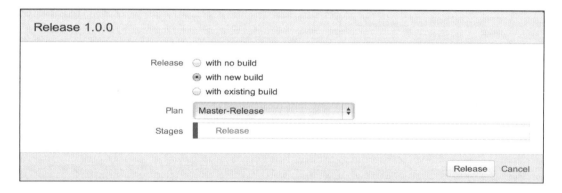

Another feature you get from integration is that you can get a list with a summary of all the builds for your project by navigating to **Overview | Builds**.

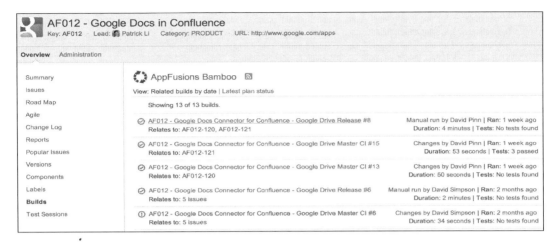

There's more...

Apart from Bamboo, JIRA also has support for other build server systems, such as Jenkins and Hudson, via third-party add-ons. You can get the add-on for Jenkins and Hudson from the following link:

```
https://marketplace.atlassian.com/plugins/com.marvelution.jira.
plugins.jenkins
```

After you have installed the add-on, there will be two new application types to choose from while creating new application links, namely Hudson and Jenkins.

Integrating JIRA with Stash

Stash is the on-premise Git source code management tool for the enterprise. It is another application from Atlassian that provides you with all the great DVCS features and benefits such as GitHub, but lets you keep it on your own server.

In this recipe, we will integrate JIRA with Stash so that developers can see what changes are made against a given issue.

Getting ready

Since we will be using Stash in this recipe, you need to have a Stash instance running on your system. If you do not have one, you can download a free Stash trial from `https://www.atlassian.com/software/stash`.

How to do it...

Perform the following steps to integrate JIRA with Stash:

1. Navigate to **Administration | Add-ons | Application Links**.
2. Enter your Stash URL and create the application link. JIRA should automatically detect the target application as Stash; if, for some reason, it does not, make sure you select **Stash** as the **Application Type** when prompted.

How it works...

The JIRA and Stash integration works by looking through your commit logs for comments that start with or contain any issue keys. If the commit comment contains an issue, such as the one shown in the following screenshot, the commit will be displayed when you click on the **Source** tab of the issue:

```
AF020 - add macro parameter description.
```

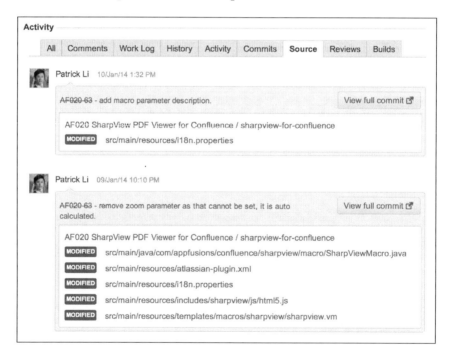

Integrating JIRA with Bitbucket and GitHub

Bitbucket is Atlassian's cloud-based code repository service. It provides public and private code repositories, with support for both Git and Mercurial. It provides a great option for organizations that want to move to DVCS but do not want to deal with the infrastructure overhead.

In this recipe, we will look at how to integrate our on-premise hosted JIRA with Bitbucket in the cloud.

Getting ready

Since we will be using Bitbucket in this recipe, you need to have a Bitbucket account (both Git and Mercurial repositories will work). If you do not have one, you can sign up for a free account at `https://bitbucket.org`.

How to do it...

The first step is to create a new consumer in Bitbucket for JIRA, which will generate the consumer key and secret:

1. Log in to your Bitbucket account.

2. Navigate to **Manage Account | Integrated applications**.

3. Click on **Add consumer** and enter a name. The name you enter here will be displayed when JIRA requests access authorization, so you should use a name that is easily understandable, such as **Atlassian JIRA**.

4. Click on **Add consumer**, and this will generate the consumer details we need for the next step:

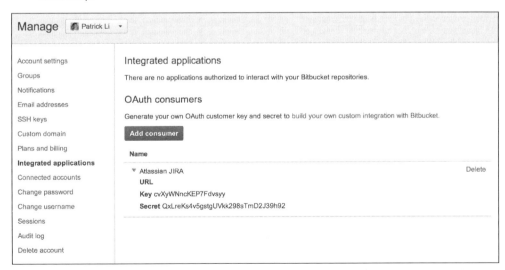

After we have created the new consumer, the next step is to enter the consumer key and secret details into JIRA:

1. Navigate to **Administration | Add-ons | DVCS Accounts**.

2. Click on the **Link Bitbucket or GitHub account** button.

3. Select **Bitbucket** as the **Host** option.

4. Enter the Bitbucket account name, the key, and the secret details generated from the consumer we just created.

5. Click on **Add** to link JIRA to Bitbucket.

Once JIRA has established a connection to Bitbucket, you will be prompted to grant JIRA access to your Bitbucket account. Make sure the consumer name (in bold) is the same as the consumer we created and click on **Grant access**:

How it works...

JIRA uses OAuth as the authorization mechanism to retrieve data from Bitbucket. With OAuth, the application that retrieves data is called the **consumer**, and the application that provides data is called the **provider**.

Each consumer needs to be registered with the provider, which generates a key or secret pair. We performed the registration in our first step by adding a new consumer in Bitbucket:

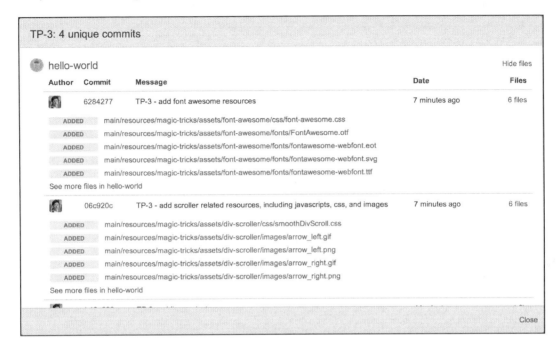

If you do not see the **Commits** tab or section, make sure you have the **View Development Tools** project permission.

 By default, members of the **Developers** project role have the **View Development Tools** permission.

There's more...

As you might have already seen during the setup process, JIRA also supports GitHub, both the standard cloud version and the enterprise on-premise version. To integrate with GitHub, you follow the same steps, except while setting up DVCS accounts, you need to select GitHub instead of Bitbucket.

With GitHub, you will also need the consumer key and secret by registering a new application in GitHub:

1. Log in to your GitHub account.
2. Navigate to **Account Settings | Applications**.

3. Click on **Register new application** and enter a name.

4. Enter JIRA's URL for both **Homepage URL** and **Authorization callback URL**.

5. Click on **Register application**.

After you have registered the application, a new client key and secret pair will be generated for JIRA to use.

Integrating JIRA with HipChat

HipChat is a group chat, an IM service from Atlassian. It provides features such as persistent chat rooms and drag-and-drop file sharing, with support for web, desktop, and mobile.

In this recipe, we will integrate JIRA with HipChat, so every time an issue is created in the Support project, a notification will be sent to the corresponding HipChat room.

Getting ready

Since we will be using HipChat in this recipe, you will need to have a HipChat account. If you do not have one, you can sign up for a free account at `https://www.hipchat.org`.

The integration requires the HipChat for JIRA add-on, which is bundled with JIRA by default. However, if you do not have the add-on installed for some reason, you can get it from the following link:

`https://marketplace.atlassian.com/plugins/com.atlassian.labs.hipchat.hipchat-for-jira-plugin`

How to do it...

Proceed with the following steps to integrate JIRA with HipChat:

1. The first step is to create a new API token in HipChat for JIRA:

    1. Log in to your HipChat account; you need to have admin-level access.

    2. Navigate to **Group Admin | API**.

    3. Select **Admin** for **Type** and enter a label. The label should indicate the system that will be using the token, for example, JIRA.

4. Click on **Create** to create the new API token:

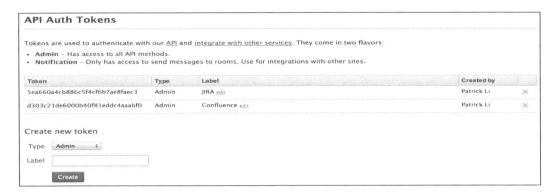

2. Now that we have created a new API token, we can use it to enable integration between JIRA and HipChat:

   1. Navigate to **Administration | System | HipChat Configuration**.
   2. Cut and paste the API token from HipChat into the **Admin Token** field and click on **Save**.

3. The last step is to update our workflow so that JIRA will send out notifications when an issue is transitioned; this is done as follows:

   1. Navigate to **Administration | Issues | Workflows**.
   2. Click on the **Edit** link for the workflow that is used by our project.
   3. Locate the **Create Issue** transition and click on **Post functions**.
   4. Click on the **Add post function** link and select **Notify hipchat**.
   5. Enter the JQL query if you want to filter and limit the issues that will send notifications to HipChat; leave it blank for all issues.
   6. Select the chat room(s) that the notifications should be sent to.
   7. Select whether HipChat clients should also be notified.
   8. Click on **Update** to add the post function and move it below the **Create issue** post function.
   9. Publish the draft to apply the changes.

The **Add Parameters To Function** window looks something like the following screenshot:

Add Parameters To Function

Add required parameters to the Function.

JQL filter to use. Notifications will be sent for only the issues matching this filter. If empty, notifications will be sent for all issues.

JQL:

HipChat rooms to notify when this transition happens:

Rooms:
- ☐ Come in and relax
- ☐ Developers Hangout
- ☐ GTD
- ☐ Project Hummingbird
- ☐ Support

Trigger a client-side notification in each room:

☐ Enabled

[Add] Cancel

 You must place the post function below the **Creates the issue originally** post function.

How it works...

In order for any application to integrate with and make remote API calls to HipChat, an API token must be used.

Out of the box, HipChat integration works by using post functions that trigger JIRA to send notifications to HipChat. Since we added the **Notify hipchat** post function to the **Create Issue** transition, every time an issue is created, a notification message is sent to the selected HipChat room.

Note that we moved the post function down the list. This is necessary as we are doing this on the **Create Issue** transition, so we need the issue to be created before we send the notification; otherwise, the notification will not contain the issue key or the link to the issue. Since this integration is based on post functions, we can add the trigger to any transitions in the workflow.

The JQL field in the post function allows us to limit what JIRA will send to HipChat. For example, we can use the following JQL to only send issues of the `Support Request` type:

```
issuetype = "Support Request"
```

There's more...

Other than the out-of-the-box HipChat integration, there is also another third-party add-on that adds more features and capabilities. With this add-on, you can do the following:

- Send notifications to HipChat rooms based on events in JIRA on a per project basis
- The administrators will be able to send announcements to select HipChat rooms

You can get the add-on from the following link:

```
https://marketplace.atlassian.com/plugins/com.go2group.hipchat.
hipchat-plugin
```

Apart from HipChat, there are many other chat applications out there that can be integrated with JIRA. For example, you can integrate JIRA with IBM Sametime using the Sametime integration add-on; it can be downloaded from the following link:

```
http://www.appfusions.com/display/SAMETIME/Home
```

Creating navigation links with other applications

Integration usually means sharing data between two systems; however, it is also important to be able to easily navigate between systems. In this recipe, we will create navigation links for applications and other resources that JIRA can integrate with.

How to do it...

Perform the following steps to set up navigation links in JIRA:

1. Navigate to **Administration | System | Application Navigator**.
2. Enter the name for the navigation link. This should either be the name of the application or the system you are linking to or the name of the resource.
3. Enter the URL for the navigation link.
4. Check the **Hide** option if you want to hide the link from everyone temporarily.
5. Select the groups that can see the link, or leave it empty if you want everyone to be able to see it.
6. Click on **Add** to create the link.

The **Application Navigator** window should look something like the following screenshot:

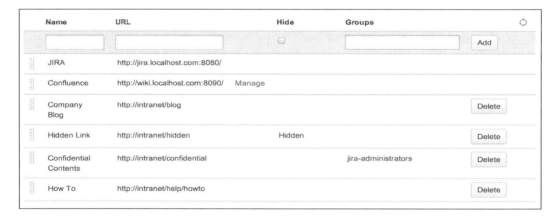

Name	URL	Hide	Groups	
		☐		Add
JIRA	http://jira.localhost.com:8080/			
Confluence	http://wiki.localhost.com:8090/	Manage		
Company Blog	http://intranet/blog			Delete
Hidden Link	http://intranet/hidden	Hidden		Delete
Confidential Contents	http://intranet/confidential		jira-administrators	Delete
How To	http://intranet/help/howto			Delete

How it works...

Every application integrated with JIRA through the Application Link feature will be automatically added to **Application Navigator**, and you cannot delete these applications unless you delete the link between the applications. This is shown in the preceding screenshot, where Confluence does not have a Delete button available.

For all other links that you add, they can be any arbitrary links. One of the most common use cases is to create links as shortcuts to specific pages, such as portal sites or company policy pages.

The links added will be displayed by clicking on the application navigator icon at the top-left corner. Note that if you do not have any links, the icon will not be displayed:

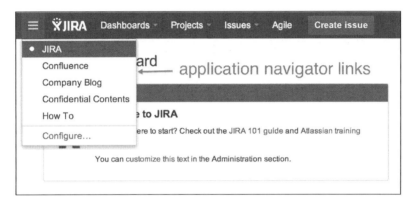

There's more...

The application navigator is very easy to use. There is also an alternative add-on called Unified Navigation Plugin; you can get it from the following link:

```
https://marketplace.atlassian.com/plugins/nl.tweeenveertig.navigator-
plugin
```

With this add-on, the links appear at the top of the page so that they are easily accessible, and you are able to set the look and feel of the links:

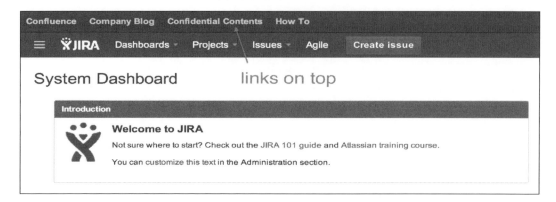

Integrating JIRA with Google Drive

It is common for organizations today to use some kind of document management system, either on-premise or on the cloud, such as Google Drive, Box, and Dropbox.

In this recipe, we will integrate JIRA with Google Drive, so users will be able to search, link, preview, and download files stored in Google from JIRA.

Getting ready

For this recipe, we need to have the Google Drive in the Atlassian JIRA add-on installed. You can download it from the following link and install it with the UPM:

```
http://www.appfusions.com/display/GDOCSJ/Home
```

How to do it...

Perform the following steps to set up an integration between JIRA and Google Drive:

1. Navigate to **Administration** | **Add-ons** | **Google Configuration**.
2. Fill in the configuration details for Google. The most important information here is the consumer key and secret.
3. Click on **Save** to complete the configuration setup.
4. To get your Google consumer key and secret, you need to be the domain administrator for your Google account, and navigate to **Security** | **Advanced Settings** | **Manage OAuth domain key**.

The following table summarizes the fields on the **Google Configuration** page:

Field	Description
Name	The name of the application, that is, JIRA.
Description	A short description of the application.
Domain	This is an optional parameter. By setting the domain value, such as `yourcompany.com`, you can force users to only address their company Google account, and not their personal accounts.
Consumer Key	The Google consumer key.
Consumer Secret	The Google consumer secret.

The **Google Configuration** page is displayed in the following screenshot:

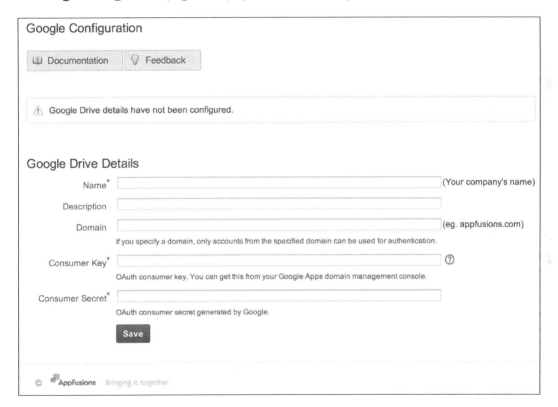

How it works...

The Google Drive in JIRA integration uses OAuth, where each user needs to first authorize JIRA to access Google Drive on their behalf; this process is called the **OAuth dance**.

Once the add-on is installed and configured, there will be a new **Link Google Document** field under the **More** menu that can be seen while viewing issues. Clicking on that field will present you with a dialog to either browse or search for files stored in Google. You can then select the files you want to link by ticking the appropriate checkboxes:

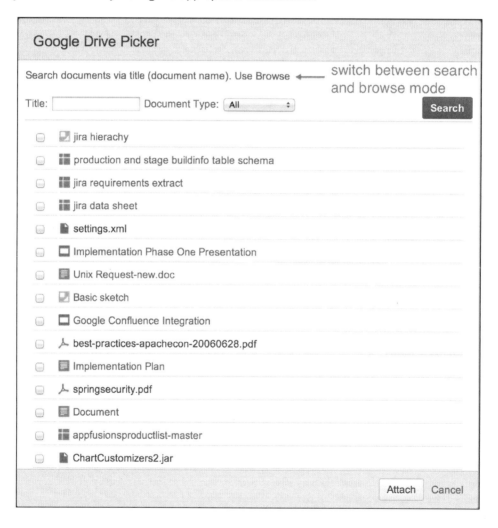

After you have selected and linked the files you want, the selected files will be listed under the **Issue Links** section. Depending on the file type, you will be able to view, edit, and download the native Google Drive files, if you have permission.

There's more...

There are many other third-party integration add-ons available that support popular cloud vendors, including the following:

▶ **Salesforce.com**: The URL is `https://marketplace.atlassian.com/plugins/com.atlassian.jira.plugin.customfield.crm`

▶ **Box**: The URL is `http://www.appfusions.com/display/BOXJIRA/Home`

Using JIRA webhooks

In previous recipes, we looked at how to integrate JIRA with specific applications and platforms. In this recipe, we will look at webhooks, a different way of implementing integration with JIRA.

How to do it...

Perform the following steps to set up a webhook:

1. Navigate to **Administration | System | WebHooks**.
2. Click on the **Create a WebHook** button.
3. Enter a name for the new webhook. This should clearly explain the purpose of the webhook and/or the target system.
4. Enter the URL of the target system for the webhook to call.
5. Check the **Exclude details** checkbox if adding data to the POST will cause errors.
6. Enter the JQL to define the issues that will trigger the webhook, or leave it blank for all issues. It is recommended that you use JQL to restrict the scope.
7. Select the issue events that will trigger the webhook.
8. Click on **Create** to register the webhook:

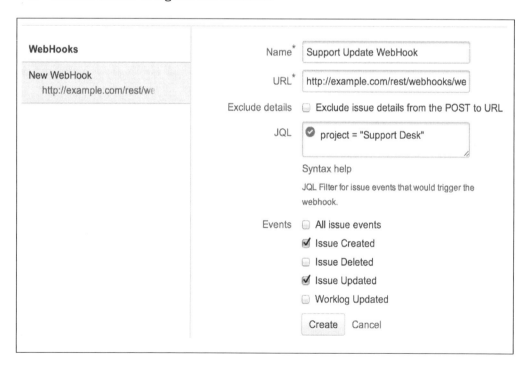

How it works...

Webhooks follow an event-based mechanism, where the source system (in this case, JIRA) will make a HTTP POST call to all the registered webhooks when a registered event occurs. This is very similar to JIRA's internal notification system where e-mails are sent based on events.

With the event-based approach, instead of requiring the remote application to constantly poll JIRA for changes, which is both inefficient and inadequate for situations where changes need to be processed in real time, the remote application can be registered in JIRA with a webhook, and JIRA will call the application when the event occurs.

There's more...

You can also add trigger webhooks from post functions with the **Trigger a Webhook** post function. All you have to do is select the transition that will be the trigger, add the post function, and select the webhook to be triggered. This is particularly useful since the webhook configuration panel only lists some of the basic event types, but not any custom event types that are used in workflows.

8
JIRA Administration

In this chapter, we will cover:

- ▸ Troubleshooting notifications
- ▸ Troubleshooting permissions
- ▸ Troubleshooting field configurations
- ▸ Running JIRA in safe mode
- ▸ Importing data from other issue trackers
- ▸ Importing data from CSV
- ▸ Checking data integrity in JIRA
- ▸ Automating tasks in JIRA
- ▸ Running scripts in JIRA
- ▸ Switching user sessions in JIRA
- ▸ Working with JIRA from the command line
- ▸ Viewing JIRA logs online
- ▸ Querying the JIRA database online
- ▸ Tracking configuration changes

Introduction

In the previous chapters, we looked at the different customization aspects of JIRA. As we have seen, JIRA can be a complex system, especially as the number of customizations increases. This can be a headache for administrators when users run into problems and require support.

In this chapter, we will learn to use tools in order to troubleshoot JIRA configuration issues that easily pinpoint the cause of the problem. We will also look at other tools that can help you as an administrator to be more efficient at diagnosing, fixing, and supporting your users.

Troubleshooting notifications

In this recipe, we will look at how to troubleshoot problems related to notifications, such as determining whether and why a user is not receiving notifications for an issue.

How to do it...

Perform the following steps to troubleshoot notification problems in JIRA:

1. Navigate to **Administration** | **Add-ons** | **Notification Helper**.
2. Select the user that is not receiving the notifications as expected.
3. Select the issue for which the user is expected to receive notifications from.
4. Select the issue event that is triggering the notification.
5. Click on **Submit** to start troubleshooting.

You can also run the **Notification Helper** tool from the **Admin** menu while viewing an issue.

How it works...

The **Notification Helper** tool works by looking at the notification scheme settings used by the project of the selected issue, and it verifies whether the selected user matches one of the notifications.

As shown in the following screenshot, the user, **John Doe**, should not receive notifications from the **HD-10** issue because he is not in the **Developers** project role:

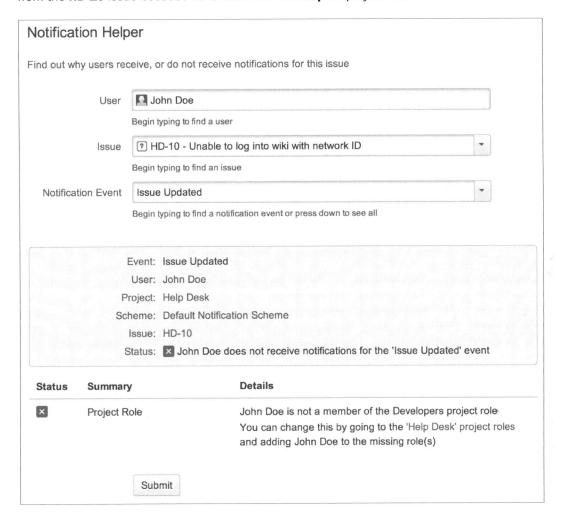

There's more...

Of course, other than your notification scheme settings, you will also want to check whether your JIRA is able to send outgoing e-mails successfully (refer to the *Setting up an outgoing mail server* recipe in *Chapter 6, E-mails and Notifications*), and also that the notification e-mails are not being filtered out to the user's spam folder.

Troubleshooting permissions

In this recipe, we will look at how to troubleshoot problems caused by permission settings, such as determining why a user is unable to view an issue.

How to do it...

Perform the following steps to troubleshoot permission problems in JIRA:

1. Navigate to **Administration | Add-ons | Permission Helper**.
2. Select the affected user.
3. Select the issue for which the user is expected to have permissions from.
4. Select the permission type the user should have access to.
5. Click on **Submit** to start troubleshooting.

You can also run the **Permission Helper** tool from the **Admin** menu while viewing an issue.

How it works...

The **Permission Helper** tool works by looking at both the permission scheme and issue security scheme settings used by the selected issue. It verifies whether the selected user has the required permissions for the necessary action.

As shown in the following screenshot, even though the user **John Doe** is in the **Users** project role required by the permission scheme, he should not be able to see the **HD-10** issue because he is not in the **Developers** project role required by the issue security scheme:

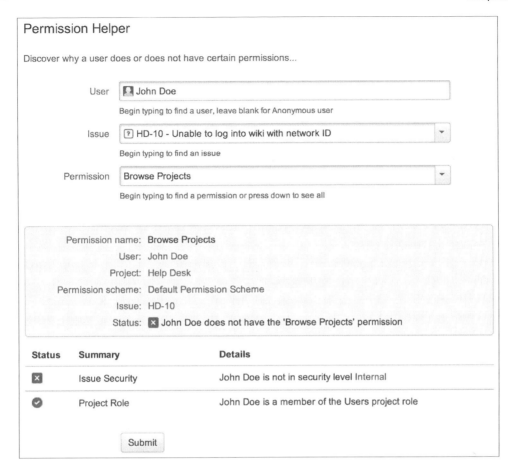

Troubleshooting field configurations

In this recipe, we will determine why a given field is not displayed while viewing an issue and look at how to troubleshoot it.

How to do it...

Perform the following steps to troubleshoot why a field is not displayed:

1. Navigate to the issue that has missing fields.
2. Select the **Where is my field?** option from the **Admin** menu.
3. Select the field that is missing to start troubleshooting.

How it works...

The **Field Helper** tool examines field-related configurations, including the following:

- **Field context**: This checks whether the field is a custom field. The tool will then check whether the field has a context that matches the current project and issue type combinations.

- **Field configuration**: This verifies whether the field is set to hidden.

- **Screens**: This verifies whether the field is placed on the current screen based on the screen scheme and issue type of the screen scheme.

- **Field data**: This verifies whether the current issue has a value for the field, as custom fields without a value will often not be displayed.

As shown in the following screenshot, **Customer** is a custom field, and the reason behind its lack of display is because it has no value for the current issue:

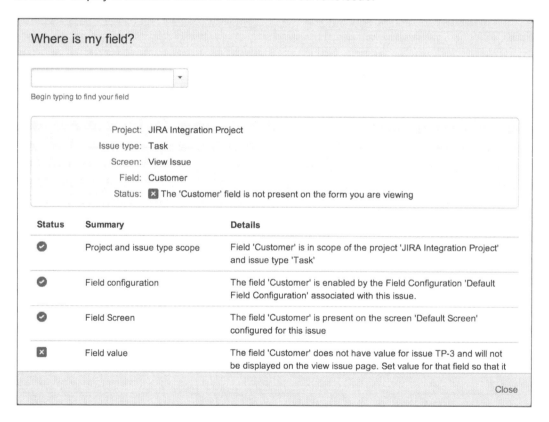

Running JIRA in safe mode

When you have different people installing add-ons in JIRA, you can, at times, run into problems, but you might be unsure as to which add-on has caused a certain problem. In these cases, you can use the method of elimination; however, first, disable all the add-ons and re-enable them one at a time.

Getting ready

Enabling safe mode will impact your users, so make sure you plan accordingly before doing so.

How to do it...

Perform the following steps to enable safe mode:

1. Navigate to **Administration** | **Add-ons** | **Manage add-ons**.
2. Click on the **Enable safe mode** link at the bottom of the page.
3. Click on **Continue** when you are prompted to confirm the change.

The window looks like the following screenshot:

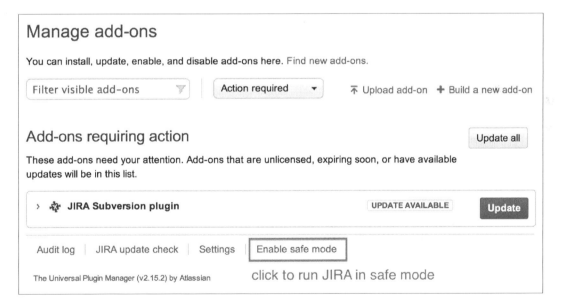

How it works...

The **Universal Plugin Manager** (**UPM**) is what JIRA uses to manage all its add-ons. Other than being the interface that allows you to upload and install third-party add-ons (unless instructed otherwise), it also provides a number of other useful administrative features.

When you enable the safe mode option (using **Enable safe mode**), the UPM will disable all user-installed add-ons, which returns JIRA to a vanilla state. You can then individually enable each add-on, thus finding the problematic add-on via the method of elimination.

There's more...

The UPM also provides an **audit** feature, which keeps track of all the changes related to add-ons. You can simply click on the **Audit log** link at the bottom of the page and the UPM will display a list of changes that date back to the last 90 days.

Importing data from other issue trackers

If you have another issue tracker and are thinking about switching to JIRA, you can often easily migrate your existing data into JIRA with its built-in import tool.

In this recipe, we will look at importing data from Bitbucket's issue tracker. JIRA supports importing data from other issue trackers, such as Bugzilla and Mantis, and as we will see, the process is mostly identical.

How to do it...

Perform the following steps to import data from other issue trackers, such as Bitbucket, into JIRA:

1. Navigate to **Administration | System | External System Import**.
2. Select the source's issue tracker system. We will select **Bitbucket** for this recipe.

3. Click on the **Next** button to authorize the JIRA importer to access data from Bitbucket, and when prompted, click on **Authorize**:

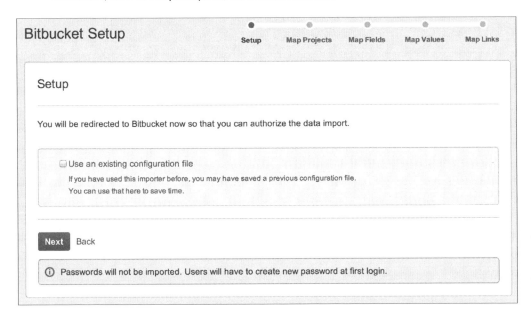

4. Map projects from Bitbucket to JIRA projects. For those projects you do not want to import to JIRA, leave them selected with the **Don't import this project** option. Click on **Next** to continue.

   After you have clicked on **Next**, JIRA will query Bitbucket to get an export of settings such as fields and values so that they can be used to map JIRA counterparts. This process may take a few minutes depending on the size of your Bitbucket project.

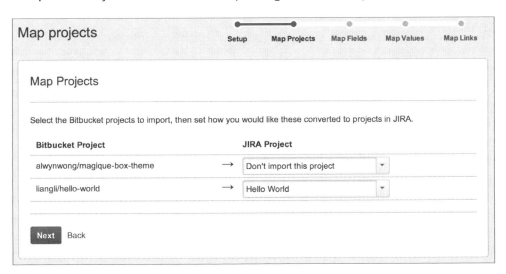

5. Select the fields from Bitbucket that you want to manually map to the JIRA field values.

6. Select the workflow scheme used by the target JIRA project so that we can map Bitbucket statuses to JIRA statuses in the next step. Click on **Next** to continue:

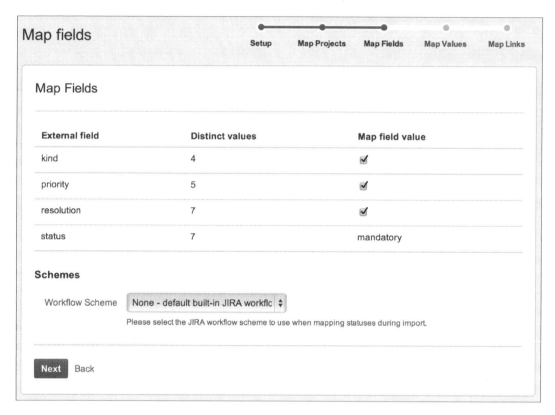

Map fields

Setup   Map Projects   **Map Fields**   Map Values   Map Links

Map Fields

External field	Distinct values	Map field value
kind	4	☑
priority	5	☑
resolution	7	☑
status	7	mandatory

Schemes

Workflow Scheme   `None - default built-in JIRA workflc ⬍`

Please select the JIRA workflow scheme to use when mapping statuses during import.

Next   Back

Make sure you select the correct workflow scheme by checking the project configuration; otherwise, the import process can fail due to incorrect status mapping.

7. Map the field values from Bitbucket to the field values of the JIRA fields as shown in the screenshot that follows. Click on **Next** to continue.

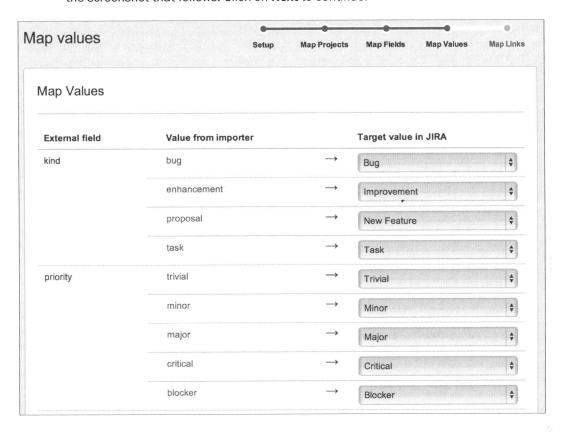

8. Map Bitbucket's link types to the JIRA issue link types. Click on **Begin Import** to start importing data into JIRA:

9. Review the import result. You can click on the **download a detailed log** link to get a full log of the process if the import has failed. You can also click on the **save the configuration** link to get a copy of the mapped files so that you do not have to remap everything from scratch the next time.

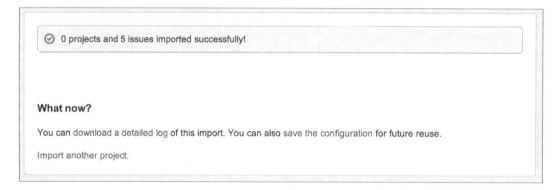

How it works...

JIRA has a common wizard interface for all the different issue tracker importers. While each importer has its own uniqueness, they all follow the same basic steps, as outlined in the following list:

- ▶ **Configuring the target data source**: This is set to retrieve the target issue tracker's data. It can be a direct database access in the case of Bugzilla, or it can be over the Internet in the case of Bitbucket.

- ▶ **Selecting a project to import to**: This is where we have to choose issues that should be imported to either an existing project or a new project.

- ▶ **Mapping target system fields to JIRA fields**: This is where the target issue maps the tracker's fields to the corresponding JIRA fields. Custom fields can be automatically created as part of the process.

- ▶ **Mapping a target system field values to JIRA field values**: This maps the field data based on the previous field mappings. It is usually required for selecting list-based fields such as priority, issue status, and custom fields.

- ▶ **Mapping the issue link types**: This step is optional depending on whether the target issue tracker supports linking. If it does, those link types will need to be mapped to the JIRA issue link types.

Although the JIRA importer is able to handle most instances where the data mapping is straightforward, for bigger instances with complex mapping requirements, such as project merging and conditional mapping, it is recommended to engage an Atlassian Expert (`https://www.atlassian.com/resources/experts`) to handle the migration, rather than relying on the importer alone.

There's more...

Other than the out-of-the-box supported issue trackers, there are other third-party add-ons that have support for other systems. For example, there is an add-on for importing issues from GitHub called JIRA GitHub Issue Importer, and you can get it from the following link:

`https://marketplace.atlassian.com/plugins/com.atlassian.jira.plugins.jira-importers-github-plugin`

If there are no import options available for your issue tracker, you can also try to export your data in the CSV format and then use the built-in CSV importer to import the data. This is what we will discuss in the following recipe, *Importing data from CSV*.

Importing data from CSV

JIRA comes with a number of importers to import data from other popular issue trackers. If you want to import data from an unsupported issue tracker, JIRA provides a generic **comma-separated values** (**CSV**) importer. This is also quite useful if you want to import data from some generic applications, such as MS Excel.

In this recipe, we will look at importing data from a CSV file.

How to do it...

Perform the following steps to use the CSV importer:

1. Navigate to **Administration | System | External System Import**.
2. Select the **Import from Comma-separated values (CSV)** option.
3. Select the source CSV file in the **CSV Source File** field:

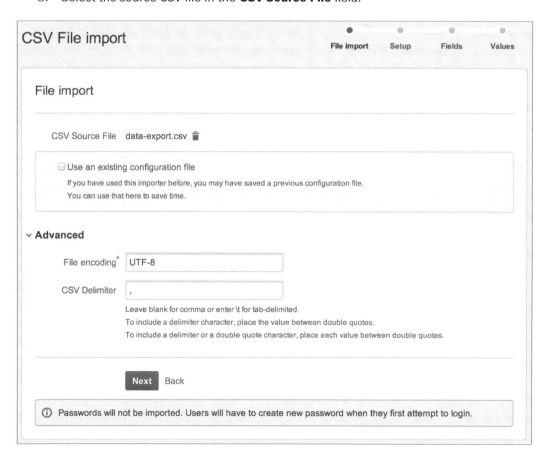

4.   Expand the **Advanced** section and select the file encoding used in the CSV file and the delimiter if you are not using the default comma (**,**) character. Click on **Next** to go to step 2.

5.   Select the project you want to import your CSV data to and the format used to represent the date. This is important; otherwise, JIRA may not be able to parse the date values contained in the file. Click on **Next** to go to step 3:

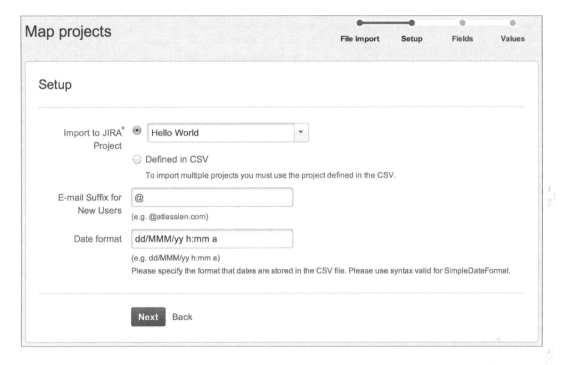

6.   Map the CSV columns to the JIRA fields. For this step, you have to at least map a column to the issue summary field. Check the **Map field value** checkbox for fields you want to map values for, such as for select list fields. Click on **Next** to continue.

7.   Map values from the CSV file to the JIRA field values. The CSV importer will use this as a mapping rule while processing the CSV file. Click on **Begin Import** to start importing data.

8. Review the import result. You can click on the **download a detailed log** link to get a full log of the process if the import has failed. You can also click on the **save the configuration** link to get a copy of the mapping files so that the next time, you do not have to remap everything from scratch.

Checking data integrity in JIRA

JIRA comes with a database integrity checker utility to help you identify and fix data inconsistencies, which can often occur as a result of the following:

▶ Installing and uninstalling add-ons with custom fields and workflow modules

▶ Direct database manipulation via custom applications and/or scripts

These inconsistencies can sometimes lead to workflow errors or even system crashes. In this recipe, we will look at how to correct these data inconsistencies.

Getting ready

Before you fix any errors found with the integrity checker utility, make sure you create a backup of your data.

How to do it...

Perform the following steps to run the integrity checker utility:

1. Navigate to **Administration | System | Integrity Checker**.

2. Select the data to be verified. Check the **Select All** option to verify all data.

3. Click on the **Fix** button if there are any errors found to automatically correct the errors.

How it works...

As shown in the following screenshot, we have two data integrity errors related to custom fields caused by custom fields being deleted but still referenced in configuration schemes. By selecting those two errors and clicking on the **Fix** button, JIRA will automatically fix the errors by removing the references.

Automating tasks in JIRA

As an administrator, being able to automate tasks is often a very important task. Earlier, you often needed to have some programming skills in order to take advantage of some of the automation facilities provided by JIRA, such as Listeners and Services. Luckily, Atlassian now provides a tool to help with automation, without the need to know any programming.

In this recipe, we will set up an automated task where JIRA will periodically check for issues that have not been updated in seven days, close them, and add a comment.

Getting ready

For this recipe, we need to have the JIRA Automation Plugin add-on installed. You can download it from the following link and install it using the UPM:

```
https://marketplace.atlassian.com/plugins/com.atlassian.plugin.
automation.jira-automation-plugin
```

How to do it...

Perform the following steps to set up an automated task:

1. Navigate to **Administration | Add-ons | Automation**.
2. Click on the **Add Rule** button.
3. Enter a name for the new automation rule and select the user that will be used by JIRA to run this task.
4. Check the **Enable rule once created?** option and click on **Next** to continue:

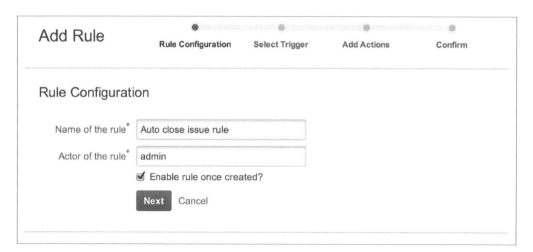

5. Select the **JQL Filter Trigger** option.

6. Enter **CRON schedule**. If we want our task to run every day at midnight, we will use the `0 0 0 * * ?` expression.

7. Enter the JQL expression named `project = "Help Desk" AND updated <= -7d`. This will get us the list of issues in the **Help Desk** project that have not been updated in the last seven days.

8. Click on **Next** to continue:

9. For the first action, we want to close these issues, so we select **Transition Issue Action**.

10. Select the **Close Issue** transition. We need to make sure that the **Close Issue** transition selected is available for the project.

11. Check the **Disable notification for this transition** option.

12. Create a new action by clicking on the **Add action...** button.

13. Select **Comment Issue Action**.

14. Add a comment to the **Comment** box.

15. Check the **Send notification?** option so that users will receive a notification with the comment we added.

16. Click on **Next** to continue.

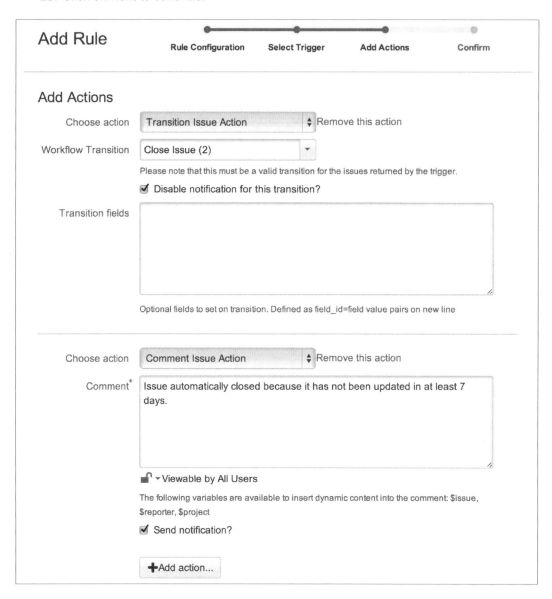

17. Review the automation task summary and click on **Save** to create the task.

Add Rule

Rule Configuration   Select Trigger   Add Actions   Confirm

Confirm

You are about to add the following automation rule. Please check all the details before hitting save!

Auto close issue rule

Status	ENABLED
Actor	admin

Trigger

Type	JQL Filter Trigger
JQL expression	project = "Help Desk" AND updated <= -7d
Limit results	
CRON schedule	0 0 0 * * ?

Actions

TRANSITION ISSUE ACTION

Workflow Transition	jira: Close Issue (2)
Disable notification for this transition?	Yes
Transition fields	None

COMMENT ISSUE ACTION

Comment	Issue automatically closed because it has not been updated in at least 7 days.
Comment Visibility	Viewable by All Users
Send notification?	Yes

How it works...

An automation rule consists of two components, the trigger and the action. The trigger will cause the task to happen. The two built-in triggers are as follows:

- ▶ **JQL filter**: This trigger runs periodically as per a CRON schedule. All issues that are part of the JQL query will be subjected to the action, provided it does not fall outside of the limit.

- ▶ **Issue event**: This trigger runs when the corresponding issue event occurs. Issues that fire the event will be subjected to the action, unless restricted by a JQL query and/or an event author.

An **action** is what will happen when a trigger is fired. A trigger can fire more than one actions. The five built-in actions are as follows:

- ▶ **Set assignee to last commented**: This action assigns the issue to the user that last commented on it

- ▶ **Edit labels**: This action adds and/or removes labels from the issue

- ▶ **Comment issue**: This action adds a comment to the issue

- ▶ **Transition issue**: This action transitions the issue along the workflow

- ▶ **Edit issue**: This action updates the field values of the issue

With our automation task, we have set up a trigger to run every day at midnight with the 0 0 0 * * ? CRON expression. We then used a JQL query to select only the issues in the **Help Desk** project that have not been updated in the last seven days at the time when the task was run.

We then added two actions for the trigger, one to transition all the issues returned from the JQL query to **Close** and another to add a comment, which will also send out a notification.

Running scripts in JIRA

JIRA provides an API for people with programming skills to create add-ons to extend its features, or to perform tasks that would otherwise be impossible or tedious. However, even with that, it is sometimes overkill to create a full-blown add-on for what may seem like a simple task. The good news is there is an option for you to write or program scripts which can take advantage of what the API offers, while not having the burden of a full add-on development.

In this recipe, we will create a Groovy script that will share a number of search filters by adding them as favorites for everyone in JIRA—a task that would otherwise take a lot of time if done manually.

Getting ready

For this recipe, we need to have the Script Runner add-on installed. You can download it from the following link and install it with the UPM:

```
https://marketplace.atlassian.com/plugins/com.onresolve.jira.groovy.
groovyrunner
```

How to do it...

Perform the following steps to run a custom Groovy script in JIRA (note that you will need to update the filter IDs accordingly):

1. Navigate to **Administration | Add-ons | Script Console**.
2. Select **Groovy** as the **Script Engine**.
3. Copy the following script into the **Script** text area:

```
import com.atlassian.jira.ComponentManager
import com.atlassian.jira.favourites.FavouritesManager
import com.atlassian.jira.issue.search.SearchRequest
import com.atlassian.jira.issue.search.SearchRequestManager
import com.atlassian.jira.user.util.UserManager
import com.atlassian.jira.security.groups.GroupManager
// Set the filter ID and group to share with here
Long[] searchRequestIds = [10801,10802,10803]
String shareWith = "jira-users"
ComponentManager componentManager =
  ComponentManager.getInstance()
FavouritesManager favouritesManager = (FavouritesManager)
  componentManager.getComponentInstanceOfType
  (FavouritesManager.class)
SearchRequestManager searchRequestManager =
  componentManager.getSearchRequestManager()
UserManager userManager =
  componentManager.getComponentInstanceOfType
  (UserManager.class)
GroupManager groupManager =
  componentManager.getComponentInstanceOfType
  (GroupManager.class)
for(Long searchRequestId in searchRequestIds) {
    SearchRequest searchRequest =
  searchRequestManager.getSharedEntity(searchRequestId)
```

```
      for (String userId in
    groupManager.getUserNamesInGroup(shareWith)) {
  favouritesManager.addFavourite(userManager.getUser(userId),
    searchRequest)
      }
  }
```

4. Click on **Run now** to execute the script.

The **Script Console** window is depicted in the following screenshot:

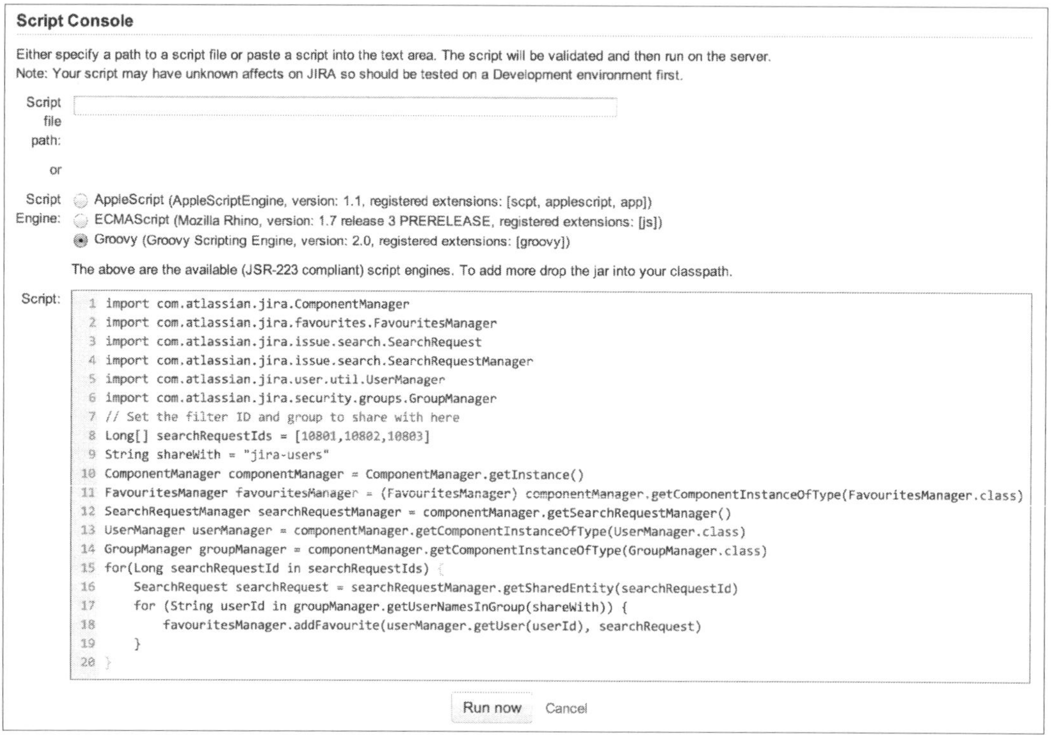

Script Console

Either specify a path to a script file or paste a script into the text area. The script will be validated and then run on the server.
Note: Your script may have unknown affects on JIRA so should be tested on a Development environment first.

Script
file
path:

or

Script
Engine:
- ◯ AppleScript (AppleScriptEngine, version: 1.1, registered extensions: [scpt, applescript, app])
- ◯ ECMAScript (Mozilla Rhino, version: 1.7 release 3 PRERELEASE, registered extensions: [js])
- ⦿ Groovy (Groovy Scripting Engine, version: 2.0, registered extensions: [groovy])

The above are the available (JSR-223 compliant) script engines. To add more drop the jar into your classpath.

Script:
```
 1  import com.atlassian.jira.ComponentManager
 2  import com.atlassian.jira.favourites.FavouritesManager
 3  import com.atlassian.jira.issue.search.SearchRequest
 4  import com.atlassian.jira.issue.search.SearchRequestManager
 5  import com.atlassian.jira.user.util.UserManager
 6  import com.atlassian.jira.security.groups.GroupManager
 7  // Set the filter ID and group to share with here
 8  Long[] searchRequestIds = [10801,10802,10803]
 9  String shareWith = "jira-users"
10  ComponentManager componentManager = ComponentManager.getInstance()
11  FavouritesManager favouritesManager = (FavouritesManager) componentManager.getComponentInstanceOfType(FavouritesManager.class)
12  SearchRequestManager searchRequestManager = componentManager.getSearchRequestManager()
13  UserManager userManager = componentManager.getComponentInstanceOfType(UserManager.class)
14  GroupManager groupManager = componentManager.getComponentInstanceOfType(GroupManager.class)
15  for(Long searchRequestId in searchRequestIds) {
16      SearchRequest searchRequest = searchRequestManager.getSharedEntity(searchRequestId)
17      for (String userId in groupManager.getUserNamesInGroup(shareWith)) {
18          favouritesManager.addFavourite(userManager.getUser(userId), searchRequest)
19      }
20  }
```

Run now   Cancel

How it works...

The Script Runner add-on comes with support for a number of script engines; Groovy being one of them. In the script, we list a number of search filters by their IDs (these filters need to be shared so that the other users can favorite them), loop through them, and add each ID as a favorite to the users in the **jira-users** group, and all done using JIRA's API (`https://developer.atlassian.com/display/JIRADEV/Java+API+Reference`).

Switching user sessions in JIRA

You will often have problems where the issue only happens to a particular user. In these cases, you will have to either sit next to the user in order to see and understand the problem, or reset the user's password and log in as that user.

In this recipe, we will look at how you can switch your current session to any other user's session, without having to reset or get hold of the user's password.

Getting ready

For this recipe, we need to have the User Switcher add-on installed. You can download it from the following link and install it with the UPM:

`https://marketplace.atlassian.com/plugins/com.tngtech.jira.plugins.schizophrenia`

How to do it...

We first need to configure the add-on using the following steps:

1. Navigate to **Administration | Add-ons | Manage add-ons**.
2. Select the **User Switcher for JIRA** add-on and click on the **Configure** button.
3. Enter the group that should be able to switch users. Leave it blank for the **jira-administrators** group only.
4. Enter the group that you can switch to. Leave it blank if you want to switch to any other user.

5. Click on **Save** to apply changes.

6. Now perform the following steps to switch your user session in JIRA:

   1. Press the *X* key on your keyboard twice.

   2. Select the user you want to switch to:

After you have selected the user, you will be automatically logged in as that user.

How it works...

We first configured the User Switcher add-on to place some restrictions on who will have access to this feature. You would normally want to restrict this to the administrators group only.

The User Switcher works by selecting a user of your choice and *switching* out of your current active JIRA session's username to the target user; it is just as if you have logged into JIRA as that user.

There's more...

There is also another commercially paid add-on called SU for JIRA. You can download the add-on from the following link:

```
https://marketplace.atlassian.com/plugins/com.dolby.atlassian.jira.
jirasu
```

The SU for JIRA add-on works similar to the User Switcher add-on, allowing you to switch your current session to another user. It has some other features, such as keeping an audit trail of all the switches.

Working with JIRA from the command line

We normally interact with JIRA via the browser. Sometimes, it is useful to be able to use the command line, especially for administrative tasks or writing shell scripts.

In this recipe, we will use the command line to create new users in JIRA.

Getting ready

For this recipe, you need to have the Atlassian **Command Line Interface** (**CLI**) tool available on your workstation. You can download it from the following link:

```
https://marketplace.atlassian.com/plugins/org.swift.atlassian.cli
```

How to do it...

To use the Atlassian CLI tool, we first need to enable the Remote API from JIRA:

1. Navigate to **Administration | System | General Configuration**.
2. Click on the **Edit Settings** button.
3. Turn on the **Accept Remote API** call settings.
4. Click on **Update** to apply the change.

You then need to install the Atlassian CLI tool by unzipping it to a convenient location on your workstation. Next, update the `jira.sh` (for UNIX) or `jira.bat` (for Windows) file to add in JIRA's details.

For example, as shown in the following command, JIRA is running on `http://localhost:8080`, and the administrator credential is `admin_user` with `admin_password` as the password:

```
java -jar 'dirname $0'/lib/jira-cli-3.8.0.jar --server
http://localhost:8080 --user admin_user --password admin_password
"$@"
```

So now that we have everything set up, we can run the following command to create a new user in JIRA:

```
./jira.sh --action addUser --userId tester --userEmail
tester@company.com --userFullName Tester
```

You should get a response as shown in the following code:

```
User: tester added with password: 89u66p3mik5q.  Full name is:
Tester.  Email is: tester@company.com.
```

How it works...

The Atlassian CLI tool works by accessing JIRA features via its Remote SOAP and REST API, which need to be enabled first.

We updated the `jira` script file with JIRA details so we don't have to specify them every time, which is useful if we want to use the tool in a script. When we run the JIRA script, it will have all the necessary connection information.

The Atlassian CLI comes with a list of command actions, such as the **addUser** action we used to create users in JIRA. You can get a full list of actions from the following link:

```
https://bobswift.atlassian.net/wiki/display/JCLI/Documentation
```

Viewing JIRA logs online

Often, when an error occurs, you as the administrator will need to examine the JIRA log files to pinpoint the exact problem. Normally, in order to get access to the logs, you will need to either SSH into the server or download the file using an FTP client, and in a locked-down environment, you will have to request this via your IT team, which could lead to a long turn-around time.

In this recipe, we will look at how you can access your JIRA log files from the JIRA UI, trail its contents online, and download them directly.

Getting ready

For this recipe, we need to have the Home Directory Browser for JIRA add-on installed. You can download it from the following link and install it with the UPM:

```
https://marketplace.atlassian.com/plugins/com.atlassian.sysadmin.homedirectorybrowser
```

How to do it...

Perform the following steps to access the JIRA log files from the JIRA UI:

1. Navigate to **Administration | Add-ons | Home Directory Browser**.
2. Click on the log directory link to view its content.

3. Click on the **Live View** link for the log file you want to view online, or download the file by clicking on it or its **Download Zip** link:

Home Directory Browser
JIRA Home / log

Back

Name	Size	Action
atlassian-jira-incoming-mail.log	245 B	Live View Download Zip
atlassian-jira-outgoing-mail.log	805 B	Live View Download Zip
atlassian-jira-security.log	99.2 KB	Live View Download Zip
atlassian-jira.log	5.9 MB	Live View Download Zip

How it works...

The **Home Directory Browser** works by displaying the actual content of your JIRA_HOME directory inside your web browser. You can actually get access to more than just the log files. For example, you can look at JIRA's database configuration from the dbconfig.xml file and download data exports from the export directory.

Querying the JIRA database online

In the previous recipe, we looked at how to view JIRA log files online, which is a very convenient way to troubleshoot problems. In this recipe, we will continue with this by looking at how you can run queries against the JIRA database from the JIRA UI directly.

Getting ready

For this recipe, we need to have the Home Directory Browser for JIRA add-on installed. You can download it from the following link and install it with the UPM:

```
https://marketplace.atlassian.com/plugins/com.atlassian.sysadmin.
homedirectorybrowser
```

How to do it...

Perform the following steps to query the JIRA database directly in the JIRA UI:

1. Navigate to **Administration | Add-ons | Db Console**.
2. Select the database table to query from.
3. Select the columns to include as part of the query, or leave it blank for all the columns.
4. Optionally, you can construct your own queries in the **Enter SQL text** field.
5. Click on the **Execute** button to run the SQL query:

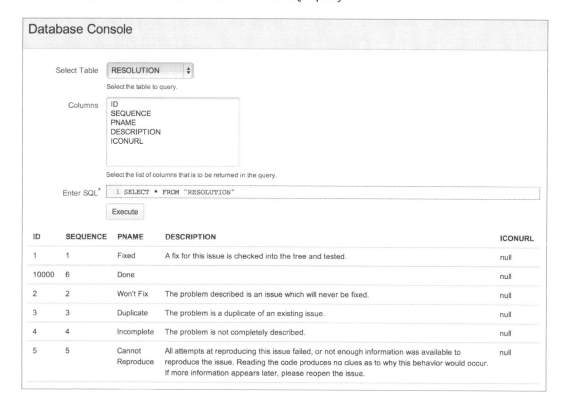

How it works...

The Db console opens up a direct connection to JIRA's database, allowing you to run any SQL statement just as if you are using a native SQL client.

It is a great tool to run SELECT queries which are read-only, but since you are allowed to run any arbitrary valid SQL statement, including INSERT and UPDATE, care must be taken. Direct data manipulation is discouraged, as it might lead to irreversible data corruption and system outages.

Tracking configuration changes

JIRA keeps track of the changes made to issues but not its configuration changes, such as workflows and permissions. This becomes increasingly important when you have more than one administrator, or if your organization is in a tightly regulated industry where audit reports are needed to ensure conformity to regulations.

In this recipe, we will look at how to keep track of the configuration changes in JIRA. Note that this feature is only available in JIRA 6.2 and newer.

How to do it...

We first need to enable the auditing feature in JIRA:

1. Navigate to **Administration | System | Audit Settings**.
2. Click on the **Enable** button to enable configuration change tracking.

Once you have enabled configuration tracking, all changes from that point onward will be automatically logged. You can view the audit logs by navigating to **Administration | Audit Log**:

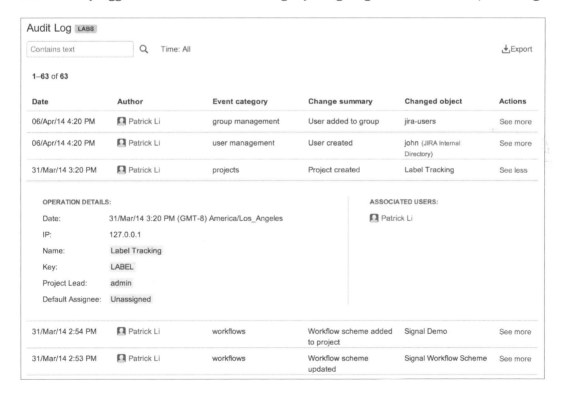

How it works...

JIRA's built-in **Audit Log** feature keeps track of the following list of changes in JIRA:

- ▶ LDAP synchronization
- ▶ User management
- ▶ Group management
- ▶ Project changes
- ▶ Permission changes
- ▶ Workflow changes
- ▶ Notification scheme changes
- ▶ Screen changes
- ▶ Custom field changes

There is a third-party add-on available for older versions of JIRA called JIRA Auditor. You can download the add-on from the following link:

```
https://marketplace.atlassian.com/plugins/com.plugenta.jiraauditor
```

9
JIRA Customizations

In this chapter, we will cover:

- ▶ Creating new issue types
- ▶ Setting up different issue types for projects
- ▶ Creating new resolutions
- ▶ Creating new priorities
- ▶ Adding language support for the JIRA interface
- ▶ Using the InProduct translation
- ▶ Translating JIRA contents
- ▶ Cloning JIRA projects
- ▶ Migrating JIRA configurations
- ▶ Creating announcements in JIRA
- ▶ Managing shared filters and dashboards in JIRA

Introduction

In previous chapters, we have covered most of JIRA's customizations, including custom fields, workflows, and notifications. In this chapter, we will learn about other customizations, including setting up custom issue types, priorities, and resolution values. We will also look at how to improve JIRA's usability through translation. And lastly, we will explore options to improve the IT process through cloning JIRA projects and migrating JIRA configurations.

Creating new issue types

JIRA comes with a number of issue types out of the box designed for software project management. In this recipe, we will look at creating custom issue types.

How to do it...

Proceed with the following steps to create a new issue type:

1. Navigate to **Administration | Issues | Issue Types**.
2. Click on the **Add Issue Type** button.
3. Enter the name for the new issue type.
4. Select whether the issue type will be **standard** (a normal issue) or **sub-task** (needs to have a parent issue).
5. Set an icon for the issue type. You can either click on the **select image** link, select an existing icon, or type in a full URL to a custom icon.
6. Click on **Add** to create the new issue type.

 You can place custom icons in the JIRA_INSTALL/ atlassian-jira/images/icons/issuetypes directory. The icon files need to be 16 pixels by 16 pixels in size.

The following screenshot shows how to create a new issue:

Add Issue Type

Name*	Incident
Description	A system outage, such as server crash or network error.
Type	⦿ Standard Issue Type
	◯ Sub-Task Issue Type
Icon URL*	/images/icons/issuetypes/exclamation [select image]
	(relative to the JIRA web application e.g /images/icons OR starting with http://)

Add   Cancel

Setting up different issue types for projects

In the previous recipe, we looked at creating new issue types. In this recipe, we will look at how to manage the issue types so that each project can have its own set of issue types.

Getting ready

Please refer to the previous recipe, *Creating new issue types*, for details on creating your own custom issue types in JIRA.

How to do it...

Proceed with the following steps to set up a project-specific issue type list:

1. Navigate to **Administration | Issues | Issue Type Schemes**.
2. Click on the **Add Issue Type Scheme** button.
3. Enter the name for the new issue type scheme.

4. Add issue types to the scheme by dragging them from right to left.

5. Select the default issue type.

6. Click on the **Save** button to create the new scheme, as shown in the following screenshot:

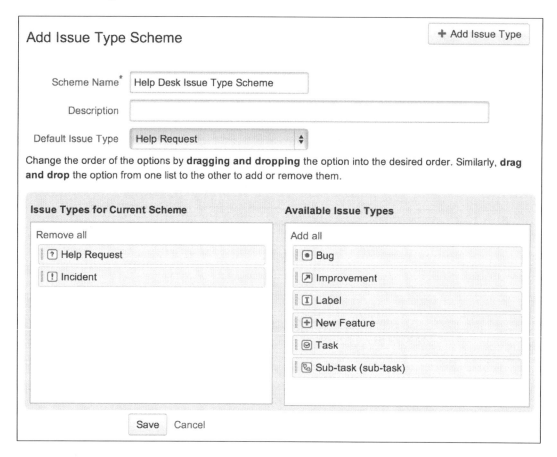

Having created our new issue type scheme, we now need to apply it to projects with which we want to restrict issue type selections:

1. Click on the **Associate** link for the new issue type scheme.

2. Select the project(s) we want to apply the scheme to.

3. Click on **Associate** to change the selected projects' issue type scheme.

If the project has issues with issue types that do not exist in the new issue type scheme, JIRA will walk you through a migration process where you can update the issue type for all the impacted issues.

Creating new resolutions

In this recipe, we will look at how to create custom resolution values for when users resolve and close issues.

How to do it...

Proceed with the following steps to create new resolutions:

1. Navigate to **Administration | Issues | Resolutions**.
2. Enter the new resolution's name.
3. Click on **Add** to create the new resolution.

There's more...

Resolutions are global, which means all projects and issue types will have the same list of resolution options. However, since you can only set resolution values during a workflow transition, you can include/exclude specific resolutions with the `jira.field.resolution.include` transition variable. For example, if we want to limit the resolutions to Fixed and Won't Fix only, we will set the variable's value to 1,2.

Creating new priorities

In this recipe, we will look at how to create custom priorities.

How to do it...

Proceed with the following steps to create new priorities in JIRA:

1. Navigate to **Administration | Issues | Priorities**.
2. Enter the new priority's name.
3. Set an icon for the issue type. You can either click on the **select image** link, select an existing icon, or type in a full URL to a custom icon.
4. Select a color for the priority. The color will be used when you export issues to Excel.
5. Click on the **Add** button to create the new priority.

 Priorities are global, and newly created priorities will be available to all projects.

Adding language support for the JIRA interface

If you are using JIRA in a multilingual environment, or if English is not the native language spoken in your country, you would want to internationalize your JIRA so users speaking different languages will be able to feel right at home.

In this recipe, we will make Simplified Chinese the default language for our JIRA instance.

Getting ready...

For this recipe, we need to have the JIRA Chinese Simplified language pack add-on installed. You can download it from the following link and install it with the Universal Plugin Manager:

```
https://marketplace.atlassian.com/plugins/tac.jira.languages.zh_CN
```

How to do it...

Once you have downloaded and installed the Chinese Simplified language pack, proceed with the following steps to make it available to users by default:

1. Navigate to **Administration** | **System** | **General Configuration**.
2. Click on the **Edit Settings** button.
3. Select the Chinese Simplified language pack from the **Default language** list.
4. Click on **Update** to apply changes.

How it works...

JIRA internationalizes its user interface with language packs. A language pack is a ZIP file containing translated labels for JIRA's UI elements. You can find additional language packs from the following link:

```
https://marketplace.atlassian.com/search?application=jira&category=La
nguage+packs
```

By setting the default language, in this case, Chinese Simplified, users will see the JIRA interface in Chinese, as shown in the following screenshot. However, if a user has selected another language, then the user selection will override the system's default setting.

Using the InProduct translation

In the olden days, in order to create a custom language pack, people had to manually copy over all the required text files, look up the text to be translated in the UI to understand the context, and zip all the files back.

Atlassian has since provided a more streamlined way of creating translations, allowing you to create translations directly from the JIRA UI.

Getting ready...

For this recipe, we need to have the InProduct translation for the JIRA add-on installed. You can download it from the following link and install it with the Universal Plugin Manager:

```
https://marketplace.atlassian.com/plugins/com.atlassian.translations.
jira.inproduct
```

How to do it...

Proceed with the following steps to translate the JIRA UI elements:

1. Select the **Switch off Translation** option from the user profile menu.

2. Hover your mouse over the UI element that you want to translate and click on the **Translate this** button. Note that not all elements can be translated. If you do not see a **Translate this** button, it means the text cannot be translated.

3. Enter the translation in the **Translated message** text area.

4. Click on **Save** to create the translation. The following screenshot shows a translation add-on page:

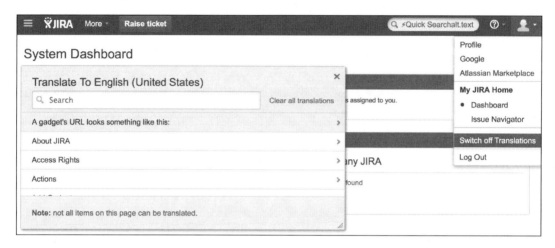

You can also search for text strings directly from the translation panel and translate the text. Not all text can be translated in JIRA; if you hover your mouse pointer over an item that does not turn green, it means it cannot be translated. Generally, most of the UI elements are translatable.

How it works...

The translations you create will be for the language you have set in your own user profile. Once you have created your translations, users using the same language for their profile will see the updated translations.

There's more...

By default, the InProduct translation for the JIRA add-on lets everyone create translations. This can be a very useful way to crowd source the translation rather than relying on an individual, such as the administrator, alone. However, you can also restrict access to translations by group:

1. Navigate to **Administration | Issues | Access Management**.

2. Select the groups that should have access.

3. Click on **Apply** to restrict access.

You can also review the translations you have and package them as a language pack. You can then deploy this to your other JIRA instances as follows:

1. Navigate to **Administration | Issues | Translations**.

2. Click on the **Download As Language Pack** link to generate your language pack's `.jar` file, as shown in the following screenshot:

Showing translated items for - English (United States)

Key	Message	Operations
collector.plugin.title	Ticket Collectors	Delete
webfragments.admin.menu.section.issue.features	Ticket Features	Delete
admin.menu.globalsettings.issue.linking	Ticket Linking	Delete
webfragments.admin.menu.section.issue.attributes	Ticket Attributes	Delete
admin.menu.issuesettings.issue.types.schemes	Ticket Type Schemes	Delete
alt.text.createnewissue	Raise ticket	Delete
my.jira.home.set.issue.navigator.label	Ticket Navigator	Delete

Download As Language Pack | Request TAC Upload

Another good use of a language pack is to customize terminologies used in JIRA, rather than go for translation. For example, if you are using JIRA as a general purpose ticketing system, you might want to change all occurrences of the word "issue" to "ticket", to avoid confusion. In this case, you can create a language pack that simply changes that one word, as shown in the previous screenshot, where we have changed terms such as **Issue Linking** to **Ticket Linking**.

Translating JIRA contents

Most language packs also include translations for built-in configuration components, such as priorities and resolutions; but for custom-created options, we will need to translate them ourselves. Note that JIRA allows you to translate the following configuration options:

▶ Issue types

▶ Workflow statuses

▶ Priorities

▶ Resolutions

▶ Custom field names (not options)

In this recipe, we will look at translating priority values.

How to do it...

Proceed with the following steps to translate priorities:

1. Navigate to **Administration | Issues | Priorities**.
2. Click on the **Translate priorities** link.
3. Select the language you want to translate priority values to.
4. Enter the translated text.
5. Click on **Update** to save the translations.

You can also translate other components such as resolutions and custom field names in the same way.

There's more...

Other than the configuration options, you can also translate user-generated content such as issue summaries and descriptions on the fly, using an add-on called Speak My Language for JIRA. You can download it from the following link:

```
http://www.appfusions.com/display/SPLMYLJ/Home
```

Once you have installed the add-on, there will be a new **Translate** button on the **View Issue** screen. Users will be able to select the language and all issue contents will be translated on the fly, as shown in the following screenshot; the issue summary and other field contents are translated to German:

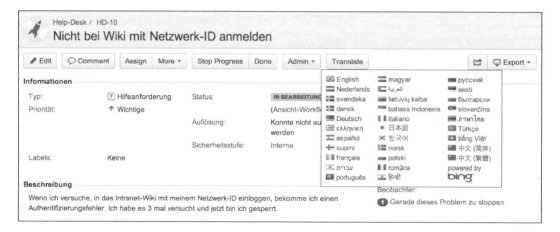

Cloning JIRA projects

If you need to create many projects, sometimes it is much easier to clone an existing template project rather than create new ones from scratch, especially if all projects will have a long list of similar components and versions.

In this recipe, we will look at how to clone an existing project.

Getting ready...

For this recipe, we need to have the Clone Project for JIRA add-on installed. You can download it from the following link and install it with the Universal Plugin Manager:

```
https://marketplace.atlassian.com/plugins/com.atlassian.jira.plugins.
jira-clone-project-plugin
```

How to do it...

Proceed with the following steps to clone a project:

1. Navigate to the project we want to clone.
2. Click on the **Administration** tab.
3. Select the **Clone Project** option from the **Actions** menu.
4. Enter the **Name**, **Key**, and **Project Lead** fields for the new project.
5. Click on the **Add** button to clone the project as shown in the following screenshot:

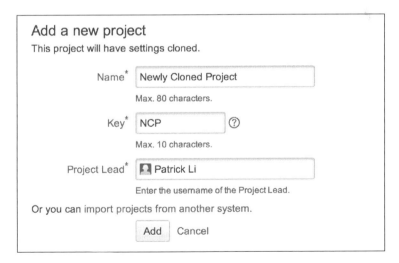

How it works...

When a project is cloned, the add-on will copy over all the relevant configuration items, including:

▸ **Assignee type**: This consists of the default assignee setting.

▸ **Project components**: This consists of the list of components.

▸ **Project versions**: This consists of the list of versions.

▸ **Project roles**: This consists of project role mappings.

▸ **Configuration schemes**: This consists of schemes such as the issue type scheme and workflow scheme. The schemes themselves are not copied; the new project will simply have the same set of schemes applied as the template project.

Migrating JIRA configurations

If you have a controlled IT environment where changes need to go through development, testing/staging, and then production processes, then without a doubt, you would know how painful it is to promote JIRA configuration changes across different environments. Since JIRA does not provide a way to export configurations out of the box, all changes will need to be manually applied to each environment, which is both time consuming and error prone.

In this recipe, we will look at two options that can help to make this process easier.

Getting ready

For this recipe, we need to have the Project Configurator add-on and the Configuration Manager for JIRA add-on installed. You can download them from the following links and install them with the Universal Plugin Manager:

▸ `https://marketplace.atlassian.com/plugins/com.awnaba.projectconfigurator.projectconfigurator`

▸ `https://marketplace.atlassian.com/plugins/com.botronsoft.jira.configurationmanager`

How to do it...

We will start with the Project Configurator add-on. We first need to create an export file of our project configurations:

1. Navigate to the project from which configurations are to be exported.

2. Click on the **Administration** tab.

3. Click on the **Advanced export** link. You can also click on the **Export configuration** link to quickly export everything.

4. Check the **Filter unused custom fields?** option as we do not want to copy over irrelevant configurations.

5. Set both **User export options** and **Group export options** to **Ignore invalid users** and **Ignore invalid groups**, respectively, as shown in the following screenshot.

6. Click on the **Export** button to generate the export XML file. Have a look at the following screenshot:

Now that we have our XML output file, we can import it into another JIRA instance as follows:

1. Navigate to **Administration | Add-ons | Load project configuration**.

2. Select the XML output file.

3. Check the **Apply changes?** option.

4. Click on the **Project configuration file upload** button to start the import, as shown in the following screenshot:

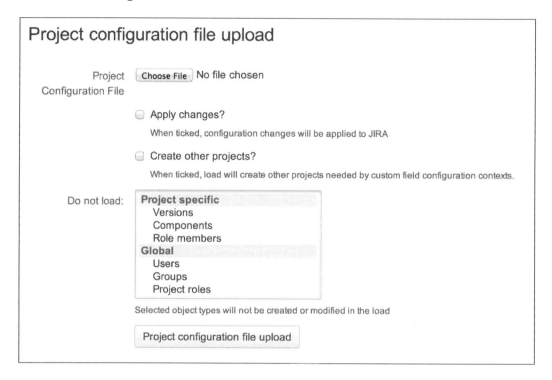

 Uncheck the **Apply changes?** option to simulate an import. This is a good way to find out if there are any issues before doing a real import.

The second option is to use the Configuration Manager for JIRA add-on. This add-on requires you to first create a **snapshot**. A snapshot contains all the configuration settings. You can create two types of snapshots:

▶ **System**: This includes *all* configurations in JIRA

▶ **Project**: This includes only the necessary configurations for the selected project

Proceed with the following steps to create a configuration snapshot:

1. Navigate to **Administration | Configuration Management | Snapshots**.

2. Click on the **Add Snapshot** button.

3. Select to create either a **System Configuration** or **Project Configuration** snapshot.

4. Enter a name for the snapshot.

5. Click on the **Create** button. The following screenshot shows the details of the snapshot we created:

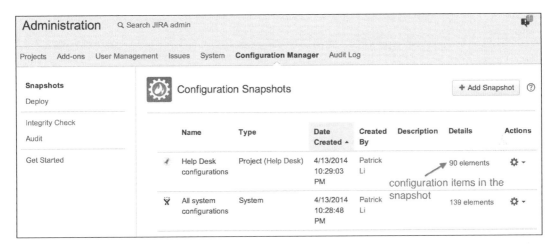

Having created the snapshot, there are several ways in which we can promote and deploy the changes to another JIRA instance. We can either download the snapshot XML file and upload it, or link the two JIRA instances together with Application Link and load the snapshot remotely. We will use the snapshot file option in this recipe.

Proceed with the following steps to deploy a snapshot:

1. Navigate to **Administration | Configuration Management | Deploy**.

2. Select the **From Snapshot File** option.

3. Choose the snapshot XML file.

4. Click on the **Deploy** link to start deployment.

The add-on will walk you through a deployment wizard, where it will analyze the contents from the snapshot and determine if your current JIRA system meets all the necessary requirements. For example, in the following screenshot, it has informed us that there is an add-on version mismatch:

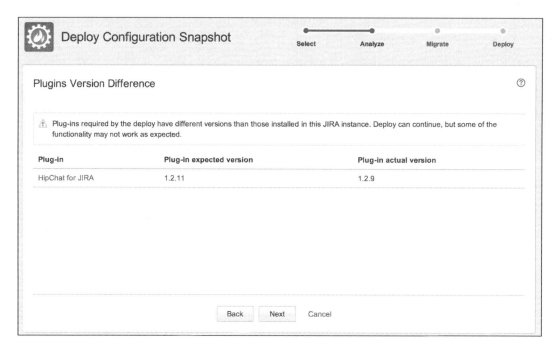

After the add-on has determined that all the requirements are met, it will provide a quick summary of all the changes that will be applied (seen in the following screenshot). This is a good time to review the list of items to make sure we are not introducing unwanted changes accidentally. If everything looks good, we can go through and complete the deployment. Have a look at the following screenshot:

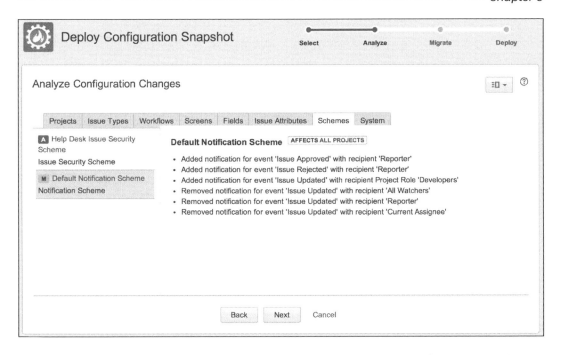

Creating announcements in JIRA

This recipe shows you how to create system announcements in JIRA to display important messages to users.

How to do it...

Perform the following steps to add an announcement message in JIRA:

1. Navigate to **Administration | System | Announcement Banner**.

2. Enter the following announcement message (you can use any valid HTML, CSS, and JavaScript):

```
<div class="aui-message warning">
    <span class="aui-icon icon-warning"></span>
    <p>JIRA will be down on <b>Friday 7PM</b> for a planned
    upgrade. Please make sure you save all your work.</p>
</div>
```

3. Select whether the message will be private (only shown to logged-in users) or public.

4. Click on **Set Banner** to create the announcement:

There's more...

The built-in system announcement feature is simple and handy to create ad-hoc announcement messages. Since you can use any valid HTML tags, you need to make sure you close your tags properly. Otherwise, this can lead to JIRA being unable to render its pages correctly. When this happens, you can remove the announcement content directly from the database with the following SQL statements:

```
select pt.id, pt.propertyvalue from propertytext pt join
propertyentry pe on pt.id=pe.id where
pe.property_key='jira.alertheader';
update propertytext set propertyvalue='' where id='<id from
above>';
```

There is an add-on called Public Announcement Service for JIRA which provides you with more intelligence. For example, you can schedule announcements ahead of time and let the system display them when the time comes, and you can set expiry dates on announcements and the system will automatically take them down at the right time. You can download the add-on from the following link:

```
https://marketplace.atlassian.com/plugins/com.atlassian.pas
```

To use the add-on's advanced announcement management features, perform the following steps:

1. Navigate to **Administration | System | Public Announcement Service**.

2. Set the start time for the announcement. This is the time for the announcement to start appearing.

3. Set the end time for the announcement. This is the time for the announcement to stop appearing.

4. Set the announcement message.

5. Provide an option URL for users to click on to get more information on the event.

6. Restrict the visibility of the announcement by optionally specifying the groups that will see it.

7. Click on the **Schedule** button to schedule the announcement.

Once scheduled, JIRA will automatically display the announcement as per its start time. For example, as shown in the following screenshot, the scheduled **System Review Meeting** announcement will be displayed on April 8, 2014:

Public Announcement Service Configuration

Start Time*	2014/04/11	✔ *Fri Apr 11 2014 00:00:00 GMT-0700 (PDT)*
	e.g. "now", "tomorrow", "2014/01/01 10:35"	
End Time*	+1day	✔ *Mon Apr 14 2014 00:00:00 GMT-0700 (PDT)*
	e.g. "now + 2h", "5:30 PM", "+2days", "2014/02/01 6:30 PM"	
Message*	JIRA 6.2 upgrade	
"More info" URL		
Target groups		
	Leave empty to target all users	

Schedule

Scheduled announcements

Start Time	End Time	Message	Target groups	Creator	Actions
2014/04/08 00:00	2014/04/20 00:00	System review meeting	jira-administrators	admin	Delete

When JIRA displays the announcement, it is in a slightly higher location than the built-in system announcement location. If you have specified a **(more info)** URL, it will be displayed at the end of the announcement message:

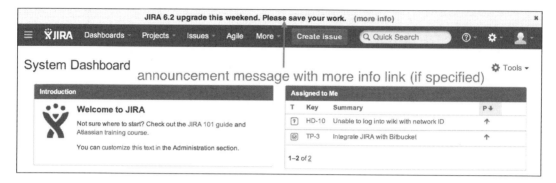

Managing shared filters and dashboards in JIRA

JIRA allows users to create and share filters and dashboards with other users. When the owners of these shared objects leave the organization, it becomes difficult to make updates to them as only the owner can make changes. In these cases, you will need to change the ownership of these objects to another user.

How to do it...

Perform the following steps to change the ownership for shared filters and dashboards:

1. Navigate to **Administration | User Management | Shared Filters or Shared Dashboards**.

2. Search for the filter or dashboard.

3. Select the **Change Owner** option for the filter/dashboard.

4. Choose the new owner and click on **Change Owner**.

 You will only see the filters and dashboards that are shared with other people in this interface.

Index

e-mail
about 138
incoming e-mails processing, with mail
    handlers 151-155
sending, to users 140
exports, JIRA
anonymizing 31, 32

F

field
hiding, from view 41, 42
required, making 38, 39
field configurations
about 38
creating 44, 45
troubleshooting 189, 190
Field Helper tool 190
field-related configurations, Field Helper tool
field configuration 190
field context 190
field data 190
screens 190
field renderer
selecting 42, 43
field required
making, during workflow transition 79, 80
Forward Email parameter 153
From address 155

G

Git 169
GitHub
about 157
JIRA, integrating with 171
global scheme 38
global transitions
about 67
creating 68
using 68, 69
Google Drive
about 157
JIRA, integrating with 178-181
Google Drive, in Atlassian JIRA add-on
URL 178
Groovy scripting
URL 55, 81

group membership
managing 94, 95
groups
about 93
creating 94
granting, with administrator access 115
JIRA access, granting to 114
managing 94
users, adding to 94

H

help tips
adding, to custom fields 51-53
HipChat
about 172
JIRA, integrating with 172-174
URL 172
HipChat, for JIRA
URL 172
Home Directory, for JIRA
URL, for downloading 212
HTML template 147
HTTP over SSL (HTTPS) 19
Hudson 167

I

IBM Sametime
about 175
URL 175
InProduct translation
using 223, 224
installation, JIRA
for production use 6-13
installation, SSL certificates
from applications 24, 25
installer
JIRA, upgrading with 14-16
integrity checker utility
running 200
issue event trigger 206
issue-level permissions
setting up 119-123
issue operations
permission schemes, setting up for 118
issue trackers
data, importing from 192-197

project role membership
  about 97
  managing 98
project roles
  about 96
  managing 96, 97
project-specific From address
  setting up 156
project-specific issue type list
  setting up 219, 220
provider 170
Public Announcement Service 234
public user sign up
  enabling 92

R

remember me cookies
  duration, modifying of 133, 134
Remote access API
  enabling, in Confluence 162
Remote API
  enabling, from JIRA 211, 212
reportercreate permission type 125
required fields 38
resolution values
  restricting, in transition 77, 78

S

safe mode
  JIRA, running in 191, 192
Salesforce.com
  URL 181
screens
  adding, to workflow transitions 65
  creating 45-48
Script Runner add-on
  about 209
  URL 55
scripts
  running, in JIRA 206-208
Script Validator
  working 83
security 113

select options
  creating, for projects 36-38
Seraph framework
  URL 134
Service Principle Name (SPN) 110
session.validationinterval parameter 109
Set Issue Security permission 122
shared filters ownership, JIRA
  changing 236
sign up
  user, inviting to 89, 90
snapshot
  about 230
  configuration snapshot, creating 231
  deploying 231
  project 230
  system 230
Software as a Service (SaaS) 157
SSL
  setting up 19-22
SSL certificates
  installing, from applications 24, 25
SSL for JIRA
  about 26
  using, steps 26
SSO
  enabling, with Crowd 108, 109
  setting up, with Crowd 107
standard issue type 218
Stash
  about 167
  JIRA, integrating with 167, 168
  URL, for downloading 167
statuses
  about 60
  adding, to workflow 62
  linking, transitions used 63
Strip Quotes parameter 153
Subject template 147
sub-task issue type 218
SU for JIRA
  about 210
  URL, for downloading 210
system announcement message
  adding, in JIRA 233-236

Thank you for buying
JIRA 6.x Administration Cookbook

About Packt Publishing

Packt, pronounced 'packed', published its first book "*Mastering phpMyAdmin for Effective MySQL Management*" in April 2004 and subsequently continued to specialize in publishing highly focused books on specific technologies and solutions.

Our books and publications share the experiences of your fellow IT professionals in adapting and customizing today's systems, applications, and frameworks. Our solution-based books give you the knowledge and power to customize the software and technologies you're using to get the job done. Packt books are more specific and less general than the IT books you have seen in the past. Our unique business model allows us to bring you more focused information, giving you more of what you need to know, and less of what you don't.

Packt is a modern, yet unique publishing company, which focuses on producing quality, cutting-edge books for communities of developers, administrators, and newbies alike. For more information, please visit our website: www.PacktPub.com.

About Packt Enterprise

In 2010, Packt launched two new brands, Packt Enterprise and Packt Open Source, in order to continue its focus on specialization. This book is part of the Packt Enterprise brand, home to books published on enterprise software – software created by major vendors, including (but not limited to) IBM, Microsoft and Oracle, often for use in other corporations. Its titles will offer information relevant to a range of users of this software, including administrators, developers, architects, and end users.

Writing for Packt

We welcome all inquiries from people who are interested in authoring. Book proposals should be sent to author@packtpub.com. If your book idea is still at an early stage and you would like to discuss it first before writing a formal book proposal, contact us; one of our commissioning editors will get in touch with you.

We're not just looking for published authors; if you have strong technical skills but no writing experience, our experienced editors can help you develop a writing career, or simply get some additional reward for your expertise.

JIRA 5.x Development Cookbook

ISBN: 978-1-78216-908-6   Paperback: 512 pages

This book is your one-stop resource for mastering JIRA extensions and customizations

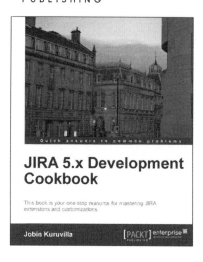

1. Extend and customize JIRA; work with custom fields, workflows, reports, gadgets, JQL functions, plugins, and more.

2. Customize the look and feel of your JIRA user interface by adding new tabs, web items and sections, drop down menus, and more.

3. Master JQL (JIRA Query Language) that enables advanced searching capabilities through which users can search for issues in their JIRA instance and then exploit all the capabilities of the issue navigator.

JIRA 5.2 Essentials

ISBN: 978-1-78217-999-3   Paperback: 396 pages

Learn how to track bugs and issues, and manage your software development projects with JIRA

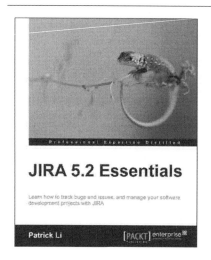

1. Learn how to set up JIRA for software development.

2. Effectively manage and handle software bugs and issues.

3. Includes updated JIRA content as well as coverage of the popular GreenHopper plugin.

Please check **www.PacktPub.com** for information on our titles

Atlassian Confluence 5 Essentials

ISBN: 978-1-84968-952-6   Paperback: 334 pages

Learn how to install, configure, and manage Atlassian Confluence 5 to build an enterprise-grade collaboration platform

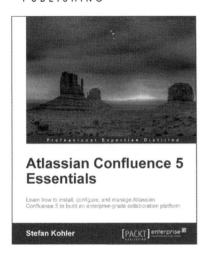

1. Create and manage project documentation with Confluence.

2. Share and collaborate on documentation between departments and teams.

3. Install, configure, manage, and extend Confluence.

JIRA 4 Essentials

ISBN: 978-1-84968-172-8   Paperback: 352 pages

Track bugs, issues, and manage your software development projects with JIRA

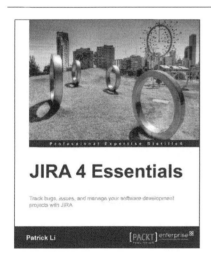

1. Successfully manage issues and track your projects using JIRA.

2. Model business processes using JIRA Workflows.

3. Ensure only the right people get access to your data, by using user management and access control in JIRA.

4. Packed with step-by-step instruction, screenshots, and practical examples.

Please check **www.PacktPub.com** for information on our titles

4037358R00152

Printed in Germany
by Amazon Distribution
GmbH, Leipzig